Port Sudan

Red
Sea

ERITREA

Massawa

◉ Asmara

Sanaá

YEMEN

Danakil
Desert

Assab

Aden

Gonder

DJIBOUTI

Gulf of Aden

Tana
Hayk

Dese

Awash

◉ Djibouti

Ethiopian

Dire
Dawa

Berbera

Plateau

Hargeysa

Addis ◉
Ababa

Rift Valley

Nazret

Garoowe

Nile

Omo

Ogaden

ETHIOPIA

SOMALIA

Wabe Shébele

Genale

Lake
Turkana

NDA

KENYA

Mogadishu ◉

Eldoret

Wabi Jubba

Indian
Ocean

Embu

Nakuru

Garissa

Kismaayo

◉ Nairobi

Malindi

0   500 km

TANZANIA

Monbasa

GRATITUDE
IN LOW
VOICES

A MEMOIR

DAWIT GEBREMICHAEL HABTE

RosettaBooks editions are available to the trade through Ingram distribution services, ipage.ingramcontent.com or (844) 749-4857. For special orders, catalogues, events, or other information, please write to production@rosettabooks.com.

First edition

"Good as Gold" used with permission from the *Johns Hopkins University Gazette*

Interior photographs come from the personal archive of the author

Author cover photo courtesy of Gregg A. Rummel

Cover design by Corina Lupp
Interior design by Alexia Garaventa
Map design by Agnès Stienne

Library of Congress Control Number: 2016958651
ISBN-13 (hardcover): 978-0-7953-5027-6
ISBN-13 (epub): 978-0-7953-5028-3

www.RosettaBooks.com
Printed in the United States of America

For Iyob Tsehaye Hizbay, who sacrificed his life for Eritrea. I sincerely do pray and hope that I have lived a good life to honor my Eritrean identity that he died for. It's an identity that I believe has carried me throughout my life in exile.

During the long years of armed struggle for independence, Eritrean freedom fighters ended their gatherings and ceremonies with a communal prayer: Eternal Glory to Eritrean Martyrs. This book is for them.

2500 BCE
There was a great kingdom around the Red Sea coast called the Land of Punt, with its center at the port of Adulis, extending to the northern parts of modern Sudan and in the south up to Djibouti.

1000 BCE
People called Sabaeans came to the Red Sea region, crossing from southern Arabia, and settled first in the Dahlak Archipelago of the Red Sea and later on the seashores and the area around Amba Soira.

8th century BCE
The Deme'at Dynasty was established in the major parts of modern Eritrea that included Adulis, Kohayto, Tekonda, Keskese, and Metera.

1st century CE
The Axumite Empire ruled parts of the Red Sea region, including Adulis, Kohayto, Tekonda, Keskese, Metera, and parts of modern Ethiopia, including the town of Axum.

4th century CE
Christianity introduced to the African Red Sea region.

615 CE
Islam introduced to the African Red Sea region.

7th–14th centuries CE
Medieval period. Rise and fall of the Beja kingdoms (western part of modern Eritrea). Some of the Beja kingdoms that flourished during that time include:
- Naqis: This kingdom expanded from Aswan (southern Egypt) to Lower Barka (western part of Eritrea) and included the Hidarb and the Mensa ethnic groups.
- Baqlin: This kingdom expanded from Rora to central Barka, and it included pastoralists who lived by looking after their cattle and camel herds.
- Bazin: This was formed by the Kunama and Nara people around Barka, and the kingdom was mainly of agriculturalists.
- Jarin: This kingdom expanded from the port of Massawa to the Barka River, and in the south it extended up to Zayla (in Somalia) including towns like the Dahlak Island.

16th century
The African Red Sea area is conquered by the Ottoman Empire.

1884
The Berlin Conference, the starting point of the partitioning of Africa among European colonizers.

1890
Italy declares the colony of Eritrea.

November 12, 1899
Eritrean resistance leaders imprisoned at Nakura Island make a famous escape from Italian troops and inspire a century of uprisings for Eritrean independence.

1936
Italy invades and conquers Ethiopia.

1941
As part of World War II, British and Allied forces defeat Italian troops in Eritrea and Ethiopia.

1952
Eritrea becomes federated with Ethiopia by UN decree.

September 1, 1961
Hamid Idris Awate establishes the Eritrean Liberation Front (ELF), declaring the armed struggle for Eritrea's independence.

1962
Ethiopia formally annexes Eritrea as one of its fourteen provinces.

1967
The Ethiopian military begins burning Eritrean villages to destroy the homes of revolutionaries. Refugees from Eritrea to neighboring Sudan reach 500,000.

1975
Martial law instituted across Eritrea by the Ethiopian military, which lasts until Eritrean independence.

1991
Eritrean People's Liberation Front (EPLF) liberates all of Eritrea and establishes provisional government.

1993
Eritrea establishes a government and declares its independence through a UN-supervised referendum, 99% of registered voters choose independence.

1997
Ethiopian attack on the border towns of Adi-Murug and Badme start another brutal war between Eritrea and Ethiopia.

1998
Border disputes result in a brutal war between Eritrea and Ethiopia.

2002
The UN commission rules on the existing border between the countries, but Ethiopia refuses to accept the agreement because the town of Badme, the flashpoint that triggered the war, was awarded to Eritrea.

Border fighting continues to this day.

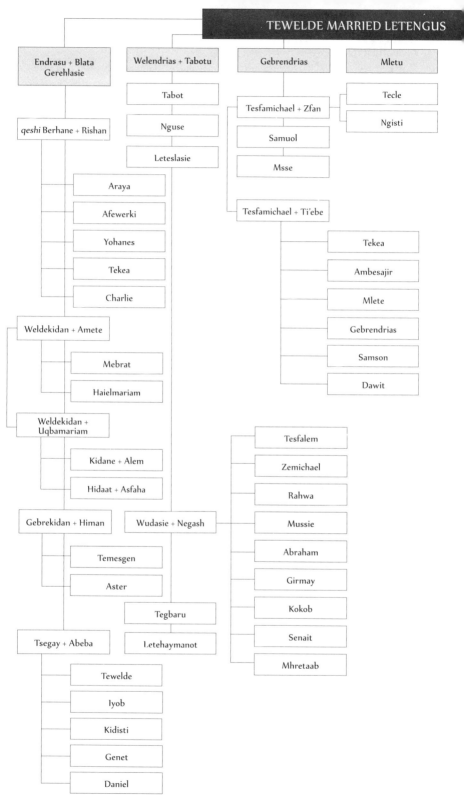

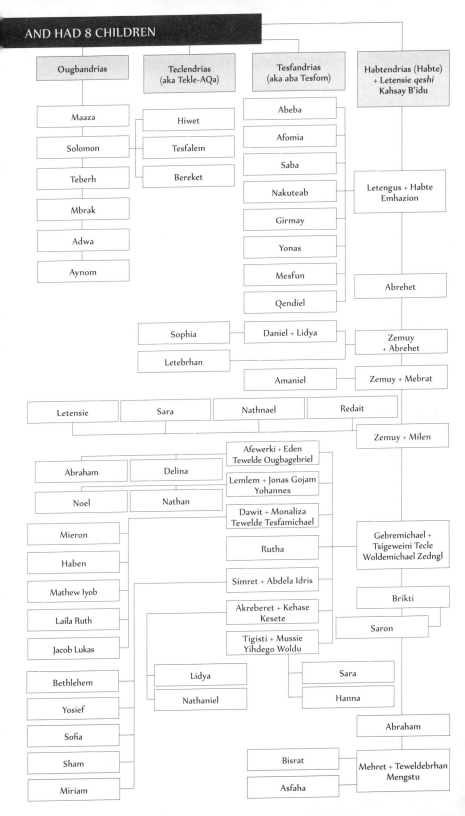

TABLE OF CONTENTS

INTRODUCTION: BEHIND THE HORIZON

"Gentleness, self-sacrifice, and generosity are the exclusive possession of no one race or religion."
—Mahatma Gandhi

Most of us dwell on the negative, yet trivial, aspects of our experiences. In support of what psychologists call hindsight bias, Professor Robert H. Frank of Cornell University wrote, "Events that work to our disadvantage are easier to recall than those that affect us positively."[1] In my case, by luck or choice, I seem to have had the pleasure of focusing on the positive. I don't know what the actual reason for my focus on the good part of the past might be, but I can safely speculate that it is because I have been on the receiving end of more good deeds than bad.

I wrote the first draft of this book for my personal use. I needed to look back on the journey of my life—I believed it would help me deal with some of the challenges my wife and I were facing at the time. Within a short period, my wife,

1 Frank, Robert H., "Why Luck Matters More Than You Might Think," *The Atlantic*, May 2016.

Monaliza, and I became the parents of three boys: Mieron was eight, Haben had just turned five, and Iyoba (Mathew) had been born a few days earlier. For the first time after many years, I was afraid of the unknown. I was scared. I did not know what to do.

From my past, I learned that all of the life-threatening and life-changing challenges I had faced were not permanent. I had been making decisions at various junctions based on the assumption that my challenges were transitional—I could always see a ray of light at the end of each tunnel.

Through the writing process, I learned that I had very little control over the outcomes and end results of my actions. And more, I observed a pattern of tremendous support from the great people I met along my way.

Steve Jobs said, "You can't connect the dots looking forward; you can only connect them looking backward. So you have to trust that the dots will somehow connect in your future. You have to trust in something—your gut, destiny, life, karma, whatever. Because believing that the dots will connect down the road will give you the confidence to follow your heart even when it leads you off the well-worn path, and that will make all the difference."[2] By writing this book, I regained my confidence to follow my heart, as I have done in the past. I was ready to raise my kids.

I continued writing and updating this book for over ten years. I wanted to follow the Eritrean adage "To those who have done you favors, either return the favor or tell others about their good deeds." Through the pages of this book, I

2 Jobs, Steve, Stanford University commencement address, 2005, https://www.youtube.com/watch?v=UF8uR6Z6KLc

recognized and acknowledged the angels without wings who helped me, expecting nothing in return except the hope that I would eventually pay it forward. I cannot imagine in my wildest dreams anything these individuals would want from me. Even if there were, I don't think I could ever afford it. What I can do is tell their stories to the rest of the world. Ande Chirum, Abrehet Habte, Ezgharia Tecle, Aboy Mebrahtu Negusse, Mohammed Kelifa, Araya Weldehiwet, Leterbrhan Fsehaye, Dr. John Dalton, Dave Rysak, Alan Zins, Biff LeVee, Beatrice Newel, Carolyn Finegar, Rose Varner-Gaskins, Dr. Tekie Fessehatzion, and Michael Bloomberg all taught me that we are indeed good and decent by nature. This book contains many names for this reason, and I've provided a family tree for reference.

I will share the story of my parents: a story of selfless dedication for the betterment of their offspring. The story of a mother who spent most of her weekdays in the village and came to the city over the weekends to tend to her children. The story of a father whose first instructions to his wife, after crossing multiple countries' borders and barely breathing the air of relief, were to take his children to the city and send them to school. At that time, my father was in serious financial debt and did not even know when he could start repaying his creditors.

I have integrated Eritrean history into this memoir in order to provide background information on the causes of Eritreans' migrations—a human face to the cost of the many wars caused by geopolitical (mis)calculations made from distant places. War is not that distant to the innocent who get entangled in situations completely outside their control.

As a citizen of the United States of America and as someone who has been on the receiving end of the great things Americans have to offer, I have an obligation and a responsibility to voice my opinion for the betterment of my adopted country's domestic and foreign policies. My adopted country has not been anything but good to me. I have grown to appreciate and admire the values and ideals of Americans. But, at times, I have observed our elected officials' tendencies to stray from the core values and ideals of the people they are supposed to represent. The unintended consequences of the political contrivances employed by our elected officials create resentment and abhorrence to our way of life.

As a native Eritrean, I have suffered from the misguided foreign policies advanced by my adopted country. Due to the number of wars Eritreans have been involved in where American taxpayers' money has been used to fund the other side of the warring factions, I lost my childhood friends and I am left with a handicapped younger sister. The war has reached home regardless of my residential address.

WHAT'S IN A NAME?

"We come unbidden into this life, and if we are
lucky we find a purpose beyond starvation, misery,
and early death, which, lest we forget, is the
common lot." —Abraham Verghese

I was born on June 6 in Asmara, Eritrea, according to the records in the Savior of the World Orthodox Church—Medhanie Alem in Tigrinya, one of the Semitic languages spoken in Eritrea and parts of Ethiopia. But my family's memory disagrees with the church records. According to my father, I was born in April 1973. According to my mother, I was born in April 1974—a year before the September 11, 1975, coup d'état that ended Emperor Haile Selassie's reign over Ethiopia. After years of heated arguments, my parents at least agree I was born in April. I seriously doubt I'll ever get a consensus on a year, so I have come to believe that knowing the month is close enough.

If it is what one does in life that is important, then what does it really matter the precise date, month, and year of one's birth? Maybe in some places it is of supreme importance, but not in the culture that brought me up. In my home, a child's birth is linked with some special event that occurred at the time, not with a date.

The discrepancy between my parents' recollections is due to the difference in paternal and maternal views of a child in the Eritrean tradition. A father generally wants his boy to appear older. That way, the father can enjoy the bragging rights of his son's manhood much sooner. While a mother, perhaps due to a more protective tendency, always wants her children to remain young longer. There is an old Eritrean adage: "You will always remain a baby in your mother's eyes simply because she has seen you naked during your infancy."

As for the records of the Orthodox Church, the date listed as my birthday could well be when I was baptized. The church's tradition dictates that a boy is to be baptized no sooner than forty days after his birth, but not much later than that. For girls, the interval is eighty days.

A name, on the other hand, means a great deal in the Eritrean tradition.

I was told there was a great deal of squabbling before I got my name. Unlike in the West, names in Eritrea are given at the time of baptism, so parents have at least forty to eighty days to decide on the name of a child.

I was the third child in my family, Afewerki being the oldest son and Lemlem the oldest daughter. It was my great-grandmother who came up with the name Dawit, a Tigrinya version of the biblical name David. My parents initially resisted this idea because the family already had a Dawit—my cousin, who was a couple of years older than me—and it is considered unlucky in our culture to have the same name within a family. It is said that if a second family member is given the same first name, the older one may suffer an incurable sickness. My parents did not want to be the cause of this, nor did they want any type of animosity with my uncle Tesfamichael's family.

My great-grandmother Itay Nigisa,[3] however, insisted on sticking with the name Dawit. After my great-grandfather *qeshi* Kahsay[4] passed away, she served the church by leading a monastic life for more than thirty years. In her religious studies, she had grown to admire King Dawit and had committed all 150 of his psalms to memory—a feat usually achieved only by members of the clergy. Taking into account that she did not know how to read or write, this accomplishment was a clear sign of her devotion to God. She wanted her great-grandson to be as strong and as godly as the king himself. I am sure she was aware of King Dawit's shortcomings, but she must have felt that the king's heart had been in the right place. To her, King Dawit was the ultimate standard for human devotion to God, and that was all she could wish and hope for in her great-grandson. With that hope and wish prevailing, the family allowed me to be named Dawit.

In the Tigrinya-speaking population of Eritrea, there are no surnames.[5] Each child is given a first name, but their full name includes the father's first name from every preceding generation. Gebremichael, my father, was born to Habte Tewelde Tesfamichael Shnedish Hadera Ogbatzion Kifletzion Hadera-Tselim… (nine more generations of names)… Hayo, our oldest known relative and an early resident of my ancestral village, Adi-Hayo. The father's first name is used as a middle name, while the grandfather's name is used as the last name to

3 *Itay* is the respectful title given to widows who vow to become nuns for the rest of their lives.

4 *Qeshi* is the Geez word for priest. My mother came from a long tradition of Christian Orthodox clergy.

5 Tigrinya is a derivative of the Geez language, which shares the same Semitic base as Arabic and Hebrew.

accommodate the European naming system. Thus, my name is written as Dawit Gebremichael Habte.

My father is the fourth of seven children. He has two older sisters, Letengus and Abrehet; an older brother, Zemuy; two younger sisters, Brikti and Mehret; and a younger brother named Abraham. The oldest in the Habte family is Aunt Letengus, who is married to Belemberas (a title given to the most senior noncommissioned army officer, who commands a fortress) Habtezion Emhazion of Embeyto. Aunt Abrehet left Eritrea and went to Saudi Arabia at a very young age. Uncle Zemuy left Eritrea and went to Addis Ababa, Ethiopia, in search of employment, and later immigrated to Germany and finally to Switzerland. Aunt Brikti and Aunt Mehret stayed in Adi-Hayo briefly before Aunt Brikti left to go to Sudan and Aunt Mehret married Teweldebrhan, who was from the neighboring village of Shiketi.

During his youth, my father was a hardworking and ardent farmer. Eritrean farmers make a living by fighting nature with meager resources like oxen, plow, ax, hatchet, sickle, manure fork, and round shovel. The Eritrean soil is dry, greedy, and unforgiving. One hundred and ninety centimeters tall—six feet, two inches—with wide bone structure, my father found success at farming proportionate to his ability to defeat nature, so he needed to be strong and athletic.

In 1966, a few years after marrying my mother, he started dividing his life between Adi-Hayo and Asmara, Eritrea's capital, where he could make more money to support his future family. He worked as an assistant driver (*fattorino* in Italian) on weekdays with an Italian truck owner named Bartezaro. Many Italians lived in Asmara, since Eritrea was a colony of Italy from 1890 to 1941.

My father tended to his farming duties in Adi-Hayo on the weekends and by taking time off when necessary. After working for two years, my dad left Bartezaro and started working with Signor Alivoro in the Gejeret neighborhood. He rented a room in the *baracca* in Gejeret and brought my mother from Adi-Hayo permanently. They started building their family there.

One day, Signor Alivoro asked my father to bring him *chiave da ventiquattro*. My dad knew that *chiave* meant key (or, in this case, wrench), but he did not know his numbers in Italian. With ingenuity and a great deal of imagination, my dad went to the toolbox containing the wrenches, picked the heavy toolbox up, and put it down next to where Signor Alivoro was sitting.

When Signor Alivoro saw his toolbox in front of him, he probably threw both of his arms to the air like a typical Italian, exclaiming, *"Lungo, che cos'e?"* Signor Alivoro generally called my dad Lungo because of his height—Italian for "long," or "tall." My father was always very clever, finding solutions where others would give up or be embarrassed. Signor Alivoro picked the correct wrench from the toolbox, and my father had learned his first Italian number. And when the day ended, true to his resourcefulness, my dad asked a friend who worked at one of the gas stations in Asmara to teach him one to one hundred in Italian.

Tsigeweini, my mother, was born to Tecle Weldemichael Gebredingil *qeshi* Gebremariam *qeshi* Habtu *qeshi* Kileselassie *qeshi* Sertsu *qeshi* Yihfntu Janagebriel Zaqunay Te'are. My maternal grandma, Letekiel Kidane Zeru, hails from Ader-Ada, a small village in the Saharti subzone.

My mother is the oldest of her siblings. She has four younger sisters—Mehret, Ezgharia, Abrehet, and Hidat—and two younger brothers, Habtemariam and Yohanes. Due to the prevailing situation in Eritrea, Aunt Mehret left Eritrea and went to Saudi Arabia through Sudan.

Uncle Habtemariam left to join the Eritrean People's Liberation Front on June 4, 1978, along with most of his age group from Adi-Tsenaf. In 1972, before I was born, he moved from the village of Adi-Tsenaf to work at the Bini shoe factory in Asmara. Six years later, he left his safe career to join the front and only served six months before becoming a martyr on December 5, 1978, at Shunduwa, Anseba.

Aunt Abrehet and Aunt Hidat both married and stayed in Eritrea.

My mother is a person with angelic patience. While we were growing up, Mom took care of my dad's grandmother, my dad's mother and aunts, and both of her parents. This was in addition to taking care of our extended family members who came to the city to shop or to visit other family members. Whenever family members came from the village to stay overnight with us, my mother made sure either she or her sister Ezgharia prepared breakfast and coffee by five a.m. By six a.m., most of the guests were on their way either to the shops or back to their villages. Mom always served anyone and everyone who visited us or stayed with us with utmost care and pleasantness. We never heard Mom utter any words of complaint or despair.

When Mom married Dad and came to Adi-Hayo to live with my grandparents, my uncle Abraham was only a few years younger than her. Considering they were in the same age range, Uncle Abraham was calling Mom by her first name by the time my oldest brother, Afewerki, was born. Afewerki followed suit. My sister and the rest of us continued the tradition. Mom appeared to embrace the unorthodox behavior of her children calling her by her first name, considering the fact that she never made an attempt to correct us. Incidentally, my children also call me Dawit and call their mom Mona, short for Monaliza, in keeping with the new tradition.

My dad, Gebremichael, and mom, Tsigeweini

My parents enjoyed their life in the baracca of Gejeret, where those families who were not able to afford to rent rooms in a compound lived. The baracca were small compared to slums elsewhere in Africa, but with similar building styles. Metal walls and metal roofs provided the main structures. Public restrooms served the neighborhood, but the area was clean because every week dump trucks removed trash and burned it on the outskirts of Asmara.

My older sister Lemlem, my younger sister Rutha, and I were born there.

I was a healthy baby until I was one year old. Immediately after my first birthday, I became very sick and stayed that way for more than a year. I was so sick that Haregu Tekle, one of our neighbors and a close family friend, asked God why he would not take me instead of all the people that she kept hearing over the radio were getting killed by the Ethiopians. She wanted to see an end to my agony. I was continually crying and my parents did not know the cause of my suffering. The entire family was in a helpless situation. My neighbor thought death was the only option to end my suffering and allow the family to move on with the rest of their lives. The neighbor meant no harm; she was being sympathetic enough to hope that my death would relieve my parents of what seemed an endless agony.

After trying every modern medication available (penicillin, ampicillin, quinine, and aspirin being everything we had in those days), Mom decided to take me to the best medical center she knew of: the Servant of the Holy Spirit monastery. The Gebre Menfes Kudus monastery was close to Adi-Hayo, my ancestral village. Being devout, as my mom was, she felt the Lord could do what modern medicines could not. At the monastery I was rinsed with holy water every day for two weeks. I do not know whether it was the cold water, the prayer, or the air in the monastery that healed me, but my parents' faith was rewarded. I am told that by the time I returned from the monastery, I had fully recovered my strength and started walking again.

The next time Mom took me to the monastery was when I was about five years old. She and I got up early one morning, before sunrise. Due to the altitude in the area of the monastery, the water is very cold throughout the year. We queued to get to the stream of flowing water. When it came my turn to bathe in the water, one man held me by my right arm and a second gripped me by my left. They pulled me to the stream that flowed down from the hill. The water rushed over me like thousands of tiny icicles. It froze me instantly. My body shivered and my teeth chattered from the second I hit the water.

I do not really know how long I stayed in there before the two men pulled me out. As cold as the area was, I felt warmth after I came out of the water. Mom then got me dressed and I went back to sleep.

Consistent with cleansing ceremonies prescribed by the Old Testament, I went through this spiritual ritual each day before the sun rose for a week. To make sure I was completely cured of the "evil spirit" that had taken over my body when I was a baby, the ritual was then repeated for an additional seven days.

With the unparalleled love of a mother and, no doubt, divine intervention, I survived my childhood illness, and my lease on this earth was extended so that I could live to tell this story.

IT TAKES A VILLAGE, INDEED

"It is not the oath that makes us believe the man,
but the man the oath." —Aeschylus

I was born into war.

By the mid-1970s, Asmara had been occupied by Ethiopia for almost twenty-five years.

After World War II, Eritreans were placed under British military administration. Despite the objections of the people of Eritrea, on December 2, 1950, the United Nations General Assembly passed UN Resolution 390A (V), federating Eritrea with Ethiopia, a country which at the time was a key ally of the West, particularly the United States.

Despite the Ethiopian government's attempt to buy Eritreans' loyalty through sinecure and mellifluous feudal titles, the majority of Eritreans stood against the federal union with Ethiopia. In 1962, the Ethiopian rulers unilaterally decided to dissolve the federation and annexed Eritrea as one of their fourteen provinces. No other country condemned this move, and Eritrea's case was considered closed. But Eritreans never gave up.

By 1975, the struggle for Eritrea's independence was reaching its final stage, or so we thought. As a young boy, I didn't know yet how my country's history would shape so much of my life.

"The Ethiopian army is fighting the war on the apparent assumption that the entire Eritrean population of two million, not only the insurgents, are its enemy."[6]

Asmara was becoming more dangerous. A curfew was declared from seven p.m. to seven a.m. But the Ethiopian army routinely killed civilians in the streets after sunset, even if the sun set before the curfew went into effect. The Ethiopians had blocked the four exits from the city so that nothing could come in or go out. Families were forced to use their wooden furniture for firewood to cook meals, assuming they had anything to cook.

The conflict was spreading, and my parents wanted to protect their children. We relocated to Adi-Hayo, my father's ancestral village—my brother, Afewerki, my sisters Lemlem and Rutha, and me. According to my parents, during the wee hours of the morning in April 1975, we left Asmara through the western part of the city, where there was a heavily wooded forest that did not have Ethiopian security. After walking for hours, passing through one village after another as we progressed westward, we turned south. Finally, we made another turn to head east. It was night again by the time we reached

6 Krum, Michael. "Energy of Ethiopian Military Regime Is Being Severely Drained by Eritrean Rebellion," *The New York Times*, October 27, 1975.

Adi-Hayo. A mere thirteen miles (twenty kilometers), which would not have been difficult to reach within a few hours if we had followed a direct route, took us a day.

Hayo stands for "united, loving, and welcoming." True to its name, the residents of Adi-Hayo have survived for generations in their small village in spite of repeated calls to join one of the larger villages nearby. Adi-Hayo's neighbors are the villages of Shiketi on the northeast, east, and southeast, and Adi-Sherefeto on the southwest, west, and northwest. Our village was built on top of a mountain surrounded by a range of hills. Most of the farmland is located in plateaus, flat terrain at the bottom of the hills and in the riverbeds. Coming from the east, once you climb up to Ksodoba, the plateaus linking Adi-Hayo with Shiketi, you are able to see our village at the top of the hill straight ahead. Climbing down the hill, you find the various parts of Adi-Hayo, which are named topologically, including Kerni-Shih (Thousand Horns) on your right and Gedena (Flat Terrain) on your left. Husa (Sand) is straight ahead. About fifteen minutes farther on foot, at the bottom of yet another hill, if you look up toward the sky, you will see where most of Adi-Hayo's population resides. Climbing up that hill will take you to my parents' and grandparents' houses.

In 1975, the population of Adi-Hayo was not more than a couple of hundred and mostly Christian. Christianity was introduced to the Axumite Kingdom—modern-day Eritrea and Ethiopia—by a Syrian monk named Freminatos during the first half of the fourth century. Christianity became the dominant religion in the Axumite Kingdom after the coming of the nine saints that included Abune (father) Alef, Abune Liqanos, and Abune Zemichael (better known as Abune Aregawi), who preached the gospel for many years.

There were four families in Adi-Hayo, though, who adhered to the Islamic faith. In 615 AD, only five years after the prophet Muhammad began receiving what Muslims consider to be divine revelations in Arabia, the first followers of the Islamic faith, including the prophet's daughter, came to Eritrea escaping persecution and seeking sanctuary. This group was followed by a second and third wave of migrants, more than one hundred of them in total. Their message spread, and Eritrea became a country split between Christianity and Islam.[7]

Based on the adaptation of Islam in Eritrea and Ethiopia, adherents of the Islamic faith are forbidden from eating meat from an animal that was not slaughtered by a Muslim who first recited, "*Bismillah i-rahman i-rahim* (In the name of God, the most gracious and most benevolent)."[8] Eritreans and Ethiopians who adhere to the teachings of the Judeo-Christian Orthodox Church are forbidden from eating meat from an animal that was not slaughtered by a Christian—the meat is considered nonhalal or haram if the animal was not slaughtered by a Christian who recited, "In the name of the Father, and of the Son, and of the holy Spirit, one God." And of course, in both religions, in order for the meat to be

7 As a historical note, Eritrea was the first country in Africa where Islam was introduced as a religion without any military confrontation.

8 In Islamic law this is known by the Arabic term *Dhabihah*.

permissible, the throat of the animal must be cut with a sharp blade before the animal dies. Therefore, adherents to both religions are forbidden from eating the meat of an animal found dead by accident or natural cause.

When I was young, I was told that Aboy Adem Hasebu (the Tigrinya term for father, used when addressing elder men, is *aboy*; the term for mother, used when addressing elder women, is *adey*) and one of my great-uncles, Aboy Weldegergish, bought an ox together—the two men were of different religions, making this an odd business decision. But neither had any cattle, and they needed an ox to plow the farmland allotted to them by the village. While Aboy Adem Hasebu was herding the newly purchased ox, one of the villagers asked him who the owner of the ox was. Aboy Adem Hasebu responded by saying the ox belonged to him and his friend Weldegergish. The villager, puzzled by the answer, responded to Aboy Adem Hasebu by saying, "What are you two going to do if the ox dies?"

Aboy Adem Hasebu is remembered to this day for answering this intriguing question by saying, "We actually bought the ox for plowing our farmland; we did not buy it to die on us. And in the event the ox dies, whoever got there in time will slaughter it, and we will share the meat as siblings would."[9] This is how the Muslims and Christians of Eritrea live side by side, peacefully and with compassion.

9   The original Tigrinya of the statement is provided here for readers of the language, who will understand that the meaning is very powerful and difficult to capture in translation: ንሕናስ ከንሓርስ እምበር ከመተና ኢልና ኣይገዛእናዮን:: እንተሞተ ኸኣ፡ ዘርከበ ይሓርዶ ከመሕዋት ከኣ ነካውዮ::

*Grandpa Habte, Grandma Letensie, Aboy Said Adem, his wife
Adey Radia Suud, Uncle Zemuy Habte*

Even though its population is very small, to its residents Adi-Hayo might as well be the largest and most fertile land on the whole earth.

Once we started living in Adi-Hayo, I did what all the children my age were doing: tending sheep and donkeys as a shepherd. This was my first exposure to any meaningful responsibility.

Life in the village meant that we were farther from Ethiopian influence. By 1975, Adi-Hayo was in territory controlled by Eritrean independence fighters. The two groups, the Eritrean Liberation Front and Eritrean People's Liberation Front, were spreading into more and more villages.

Ever hardworking and industrious, my father started trading food commodities while tending to his farming. There was less money to be made in the village, so it wasn't surprising that he was looking for new opportunities. Dad traveled to the various towns occupied by the Eritrean Liberation Front to purchase coffee beans, sugar, salt, and other food. At times, he would travel as far as the border towns between Eritrea and Ethiopia. During his travels, mainly to the parts of Eritrea liberated by the Eritrean Liberation Front, my dad was recruited by members of the ELF and became a civilian representative of the ELF in Adi-Hayo. When he traveled, my uncle Abraham helped with farming and tending my parents' and grandparents' cattle. After all, Uncle Abraham was barely a teenager at that time, attending school in Adi-Sherefeto, a nearby village located to the west of Adi-Hayo. Just like his older brother, uncle Abraham was very hardworking and an extremely smart student. He passed each of his elementary grades with distinction.

In April 1978, my teenage uncle Abraham left Adi-Hayo to join the EPLF, along with six of his age group. That was the nature of Eritrean politics: two brothers living in the same house committed to give their lives to a common goal, fighting for different organizations.

Three years after he joined, Uncle Abraham was martyred, on August 29, 1981, in Aderde, near the town of Keren.

By 1977 the ELF and EPLF controlled most of Eritrea, except for a few towns and the capital city. By 1978 the front line had reached the outskirts of Asmara. The city was effectively under siege by the two organizations.

Once the various military units of the ELF and EPLF surrounded Asmara, the residents inside were subjected to a reign of terror by the Ethiopian army. Coupled with crippling economic conditions, life there was unbearable.

Arbitrary arrest and detention of Eritrean civilians was rampant. Many residents started to slip out of Asmara for the countryside, as we had, where the chances for survival were far better. Many residents also left the city to join the two Eritrean liberation movements to fight for Eritrea's independence. Those who didn't join the fronts trekked hundreds of kilometers to become refugees in nearby Sudan or Kenya. These are among the large numbers of Eritreans who are scattered in the four corners of the earth today.

A few days before my sister Akberet was born in 1979, my dad was forced to leave Eritrea. When his role as an ELF operative was discovered by Ethiopian security, he became a wanted man. He charged two of his friends with looking after our well-being. Of the two men, Ande Chirum lived up to his promise.

Ande Chirum proved to be an angel, helping us with practically everything we needed. He plowed our land, harvested our grain, helped us with our herds, and, most of all, he defended us in village disputes, which were more frequent than people wanted to admit.

Had he met Ande Chirum, I don't think Ralph Waldo Emerson would have written, "All promise outruns performance." Ande Chirum undoubtedly outperformed any promise he might have made to my father. I am sure he promised to lend a hand if we found ourselves in need of help. But Ande Chirum made sure that we did not get to the point where we needed help. He removed any potential stumbling blocks in our path before we got there.

Peasant life in that part of Eritrea is full of intricacies. Among these are the land distribution rules whereby parts of the arable land are rotated and redistributed every seven years. There are rules governing the land used primarily for grazing by livestock as well as the tracts of land always set aside for reserve or future use. Shepherds are not allowed to graze their animals in reserve sections of village land, and everyone is responsible for understanding and following this system of rotation.

There are elections for village administrators and judges to represent the various families in the village. In all of these village affairs, there has to be a father or a fatherly figure to represent the views and interests of each family. We had Ande Chirum, Uncle Tesfamichael, and my godfather, Aboy Welekiel Semere. Ande Chirum made sure to consult my mom for her opinions. To the village assembly, he always represented her views, regardless of his own opinions. There were times when my mom and Ande Chirum did not see eye to eye, but in matters regarding my family, he did things according to my mom's wishes. My mom, my dad, our extended family members, and the rest of Adi-Hayo all respected him for that.

Grandma Letenkiel and Grandpa Tecle

About a year after my dad left the village, sometime in mid-1980, we received a letter from him instructing Mom to take us back to Asmara so that we could start school. Despite the risk of returning to the Ethiopian-controlled city, my dad was firm in his commitment to help his children excel in education regardless of any required sacrifice or struggle. His commitment was always to see his children's accomplishments surpass his own. And since Asmara had better schools, it was worth the sacrifice.

In June of 1980, Lemlem, Rutha, and I returned to Asmara and moved in to our aunt Abrehet's house. While living and working in Saudi Arabia, Aunt Abrehet had bought a house in Asmara and rented out most of the rooms. We moved into one room after the renters vacated.

My oldest brother, Afewerki, remained in Adi-Hayo to tend our farmland. My younger sisters Simret and Akberet, who had been born in the village, stayed behind because they had not yet reached school age and there would be no one to look after them in Asmara. So for the next several years, Mom spent most weekdays in Adi-Hayo and came to Asmara on the weekends.

ASMARA
(circa 1990)

Cicero
Stadium

Airport

5 km

0

Mai Timqet
(the water of Epiphany)

Department
of Environment

Cinema
Croce Rossa

US Embassy

Santa Anna High School

Amanuel
Elementary
School

Radio
Marina

Kokeb
Falegnameria

Our house

Baracca

Colegio
La Salle

Kagnew
Station

35th division
military base

Halibet
Hospital

◆ Military outpost circa 1990

0   1 km

BACK TO THE FUTURE: NEW LIFE IN ASMARA

"Your family, your values, everything that conditioned you in your childhood will influence the rest of your life." —Deepak Chopra

Aunt Abrehet's house was located in the neighborhood of Gejeret Nueshtey (small Gejeret). Asmara, like most major Eritrean cities, was built by the Italians. At some point the Italians had begun referring to the city by an affectionate nickname, Piccola Roma (Little Rome). As such, most of the houses in Asmara are constructed like the typical single-floor villas you see in Rome, where most of the real estate of a given house is comprised of a *villetta*, built in the middle of the compound. Two or three additional rooms—usually a kitchen and a bathroom—are detached from the villetta a few meters away. These are referred to as *servicio* (services), probably because the Italians generally used those rooms to house native maids and gardeners.

Our house was an exception. It did not have a villetta; instead it had five connected rooms forming an L shape, with a corridor connecting the two adjacent dwellings. Additionally, there were two restrooms located in the middle of the front yard. For the children, a sizable playground was in our front yard in the absence of the villetta, which usually takes up a great deal of real estate.

Seven families lived together in this dwelling, each room housing an entire family. Each room was four by four meters wide. The furniture consisted of two beds, a sofa, chairs, small stools, and a table. All seven families, in total almost twenty-five people, shared two restrooms. And everyone's cooking was done outside in a shared kitchen.

Since my mother knew her life was going to be divided between Adi-Hayo and Asmara, she asked Aunt Ezgharia to help by living with us. Uncle Yohanes also came to live with us to help. Not long after we moved back to Asmara, my great-grandmother Itay Nigisa, who was over a hundred years old at the time, moved in with us as well.

My Aunt Abrehet, my Aunt Ezgharia Tecle

Our first year in Asmara was very difficult, especially the first few months. We had to learn to talk and address people the way city dwellers did. For example, in the village, when someone calls your name, you reply *wohoy* if you are a boy and *iyey* if you are a girl. But in Asmara you say *abiet*, regardless of your gender. When you address someone in the villages, you add the prefix *wo* to their name (wo-Dawit, for example), but in Asmara, you just call them by their names. Of course, in the city the names get an Asmarino flavor, or seminick-name status, to sound something like Dawitom, Dawita, or Twida. The difficult part was that we became the butt of jokes by the neighborhood kids when they heard us talk like villagers. And we had come from only thirteen miles outside the city! Such was the gap between the city and the countryside in those days: very close in proximity and yet thousands of miles apart in culture and manners. While the Eritrean cities had a European flavor in an African setting, the countryside cultures had retained their African characteristics.

During our first few months in Asmara, Aunt Ezgharia would lather car oil on our hands and legs in order to soften the hard, callused skin that had accumulated. Then she would send us outside to stretch our oily limbs toward the sun. We would lie outside in the sun for hours telling each other fairy-tale stories, riddles, and fables, with my sister Lemlem doing most of the telling; we did this till our skin softened enough for the callused parts to be stripped off with a piece of cloth. We would then wash with soap, and a small round stone was used to remove more of the dry skin and dead cells. This was all done to make us look as shiny as the city folks. Learning to groom ourselves and dress the way our neighbors did was a painful experience. But after months of experimentation, and with the help of our adult neighbors, we were deemed almost presentable enough for city life.

In September 1980, my sister Lemlem started first grade at Fre-Selam (the Seed of Peace) Elementary School, while Rutha registered for pre-K. Although my mother had intended that Lemlem be with Rutha and me in kindergarten, Lemlem was instead placed in the first grade because of her age. The insensitive statement the school director used to reject Lemlem's application for kindergarten was, "She will break my chairs." We were further separated when Lemlem had to register at Fre-Selam Elementary School because there was no space in the first grade at Amanuel Public Elementary School. This made it more difficult for my mom to manage our lives. The three of us living in Asmara were going to two different schools. The schools had different registration dates for returning students and new arrivals; new students had to secure their space in order to get school uniforms that were sold at shops designated by each school; the number of textbooks and exercise books each student needed varied from one school to another; and there was no predicting which grade would be attending during the morning shift, eight a.m. to noon, or the afternoon shift, twelve thirty to four thirty p.m.

In kindergarten, we learned the Geez alphabet, the English alphabet, and numbers. Geez is spoken in the Eritrean and Ethiopian Orthodox Tewahdo churches only, while the Geez letters are widely used for the various languages spoken in both Eritrea and Ethiopia.

In kindergarten my favorite activities were swinging and singing. In fact, I earned a nickname, wedi-Adi (the boy from the village), from my teacher Memhr Mebrat, because of my silly singing. My favorite was ሰማይ ሰማይ ትኸይድ ገረወኛ ("The Tin Container That Flies Across the Sky"), an amalgam of Tigrinya and Italian words about one of the famous soccer teams that represented the region at the time. It went like this:

ሰማይ ሰማይ ትኸይድ ገረወኛ
    Like the tin flying cross the sky
ከም ሓማሴናይ ዝትኩስ ነይረአና
    No one shoots like Hamasienay
አቪቦ ቪቦ
    Avivo avivo
ሓማሴናይ ፕሪሞ
    Hamasienay primo

In this silly song, "Hamasienay" refers to a member of the soccer team that was named after the Hamasien regional administration, and *primo* means "first" in Italian.

Everyone loved my singing, especially a security guard named Aboy Ande. Aboy Ande, who had started working at the school not long before, came from one of the villages in Hamasien. Maybe he was homesick. Maybe I reminded him of his kids and what they might have been going through in a place where he couldn't help them. He, too, knew how difficult and lonely it could be as a villager among city kids. He showed me how to play on the playground swings by giving me priority. And he had my back in other ways as well. During every recess, he made sure I had one or more turns on the slides, too.

My sister Rutha, on the other hand, was calm and reserved. Rutha was of a darker complexion, with big black eyes and a great smile. Her two big upper teeth would brighten her surroundings. Everybody loved her, especially our great-grandma Itay Nigisa. Arriving home from school, Rutha always would run immediately to hug her. Great-grandma in turn would reciprocate Rutha's hugs, holding her tightly and kissing her on the forehead while reciting numerous blessings. Great-grandma would drop whatever she was doing—her time-and-half occupation was counting her rosaries while reciting the Psalms—at any given moment to enjoy her time with Rutha.

Eventually that first year of schooling, which started with so much anxiety and apprehension, turned into a great year in the lovely city of Asmara. Thanks to our neighbors, who helped us with our studies, Lemlem, Rutha, and I did fine academically. My neighbor Alembrhan Berhe had an amazing way of explaining basic arithmetic and mathematical word problems using practical examples. She would use dates, ages, household items, and prices of basic goods to explain addition- and subtraction-related challenges and word problems. It was much easier for us to comprehend when mathematical word problems were presented to us using prices of tangible items we could touch and feel.

By the end of the 1980–81 school year, the three of us were all able to read and write in our mother language, Tigrinya, using the Geez alphabet. Lemlem and I were also able to do basic arithmetic, including addition and subtraction, and we knew our English alphabet as well. Rutha was able to count without any difficulty.

We spent most of the next summer in Adi-Hayo.

It is amazing how different life in the village appears when you live there versus when you visit. That summer everyone wanted us to tell them stories about the city, and we did. Our descriptions of the various places, streets, and games played in the city were a treat to the kids in Adi-Hayo. It was highly entertaining to us as well. Without realizing it, though, we had apparently changed so much that we had to translate some of the city words and phrases. Additionally, we could clearly see that our hands and faces had become different from those of our village compatriots. We shied away from mud and other "dirty" stuff that had never bothered us while we lived there.

And then it was over. Much sooner than we wanted, the fun in Adi-Hayo ended and we had to go back to Asmara to start the next school year.

In September 1981, my mother decided that I should start working as an apprentice at a carpentry shop near the school. In Eritrea, apprenticeship is a long-established tradition for children of families that are making the transition from village to city life.

Mom asked Aunt Abrehet (my dad's older sister) to get me a job at the Kokeb Falegnameria. *Kokeb* is the Tigrinya word for star, and *falegnameria* is the Italian word for carpentry. Thus, the name Kokeb Falegnameria translates to Star

Carpentry Shop. From then on, I went to school in the mornings (seven thirty a.m. to noon) and worked in the afternoons (two to five p.m.), for three dollars per week.

Initially, I did not like the work at the carpentry shop. I especially did not like cleaning the cupboards, tables, and chairs. Mom assured me that the internship had its purpose, that in addition to earning a few coins, I was simultaneously learning to manage both time and money. She also stressed that I had to learn some practical skills, as there was no guarantee of success from academics alone. She said that if I had both academic and technical training, I would always be able to get a piece of bread wherever I went. Back then I had no concept of what "wherever I went" meant. It took me eighteen years of formal education and traveling across the globe to realize that my mom was actually applying what Dr. Jerome Bruner of Harvard University labeled in his book *The Process of Education* the dual nature of education: specific applicability (practical skill sets) and nonspecific transfer ("the transfer of principles and attitudes" through formal education). As the American abolitionist and author Harriet Beecher Stowe beautifully put it, "Most mothers are instinctive philosophers."

After working for a year in the carpentry shop, though, I started to enjoy the woodwork and had a minor understanding of the skills I was acquiring. Some of my early assignments included gluing together chairs and tables and using nonelectric tools to tighten Formica sheets glued to the furniture. At the same time, the three dollars per week I was paid covered my school snacks and other personal expenses, and that made me feel proud and independent. I soon enough learned other skills, like the different types and strengths of glues used in carpentry, measurements, and, most of all, listening skills—because all the regular employees were five to six times my age.

Since I was in school only in the mornings, after school I would go home, eat lunch, run to the San Francisco Catholic Church playground to horse around on the monkey bars with my classmate Iyoba and some of the kids who lived in the neighborhood of Alfa-Romeo, and then get to my job by two in the afternoon.

Me and my friend Iyoba

I finished first grade at the top of my class and went on to second grade ahead of the rest in reading and writing. I was even in much better shape financially than most of my classmates. Since my salary at the carpentry shop had increased to five dollars per week when I worked full-time over summer, Mom at times would borrow money from me. She would say she was saving this borrowed money for me. In general, she made sure I spent my money on useful things, allowing only the occasional seventy-five-cent expenditure for a movie and a sandwich at Cinema Croce Rossa (Italian for Red Cross Movie Theater). Cinema Croce Rossa was the theater my friend Iyoba and most of the neighborhood kids frequented for a treat of Indian movies.

As the American educator and author William Lyon Phelps nicely put it, "A student never forgets an encouraging private word when it is given with sincere respect and admiration." I received the best and most memorable reward from my mom when I came home with my first-grade report card and awards. At Amanuel Public Elementary School, there was a large closing ceremony at the end of each school year. During the ceremony, the top three students from each class were called by name to get their awards—beautifully calligraphed certificates of recognition containing each student's full name, their rank, grade, and their picture pasted on one corner of the certificate. Those who were first in their classes received three exercise books, a pencil, a sharpener, and an eraser; the second-prize recipients got two exercise books, a pencil, a sharpener, and an eraser; and the third-place students received an exercise book, a sharpener, and a pencil. The school materials were extremely encouraging and helpful to parents with very limited income.

After I received my awards at the ceremony, I rushed home to show my mom my prizes. She was in the kitchen when I came home. She dropped whatever she was doing and hugged me without saying anything at first.

Usually, when I came home from school with my test results, Mom would say, "Son, how did you do this time?" From her tone, I could easily tell that she was concerned. Mom would start searching for mistakes marked with X in red pen on my exam papers. At times she would count two or three X marks out of twenty or thirty. Once she finished counting the X marks, she would straighten her head and say, "Son, what happened? Were you sleeping in class?"

"No, Tsigeweini," I would respond. "Tsigeweini, look, I got seventeen correct," I would protest while selectively placing my finger on the questions I answered correctly.

"Of course," Mom would say. "Why else would you go to school then? I don't think you understand my question. I am asking you if you were asleep in class half of the time. Otherwise, how could you miss this many?"

"But, Tsigeweini, the other kids got a lot more wrong than me. This is a good grade."

"Those are not my kids, son." Our exchange would conclude with my mom pulling me close to her for a warm hug.

This time, though, Mom's tone was more of excitement and elation. "Grace be upon all you saints for delivering my prayers to our father in heaven. Thank you, St. Mary, for watching over my family. Thank you, Gebre Menfes Kudus, for this day." The gratitude would continue in a low voice for me to hear until tears started welling up in my mom's eyes. Mom then looked at me with a big smile, somewhat trying to hide her emotions. Mom's low voice and her broad smile were the most powerful expressions of love and compassion no amount of words could express.

Mom went through the items I had brought home while continuing to bless me and thanking God and his army of angels, disciples, and saints for protecting her family. She stared at my picture pasted on the certificate for few minutes. She handed me back the certificate and went back to the kitchen, telling me to wait for her. I sat down on the stairs across from our kitchen. My mom came back holding a plate with an egg sandwich on bread similar to a half-size Italian ciabatta loaf. My mouth filled with water when I saw the sandwich. I put to the side whatever I was carrying on my lap and took the plate from Mom. I ate the sandwich while my mom went back to the kitchen.

My family's eating habits had not changed when we moved from Adi-Hayo to Asmara. In Asmara, we ate the same homemade flat breads my mom made for us when we were in Adi-Hayo. The traditional homemade Eritrean breads—kitcha, gogo, and himbasha—are unleavened and made of barley, wheat, or a mix of both. The breads are relatively thin and take the shape of the large flat round clay pan, which is heated over a wooden fireplace. These breads are very healthy, but people who frequently ate these homemade breads were considered backward. People who ate those small, half-size ciabatta loaves, made from self-rising flour sold at the grocery store, were considered elites. Demonizing and undermining anything native, starting from traditions and cultures to the foods the natives ate, and glorifying and glamorizing spuriously imported ideas and cultures, was a legacy the Italians left behind. Anything local was edible, but anything foreign made was delicious.

At a young age we became victims of our environments. Our neighbor's kids bragged of the bread they ate for breakfast. Some even brought small pieces as a proof. My family ate kitcha, gogo, and himbasha—and made sure we finished ours at home. That is what made my mom's reward for her son who came home at the top of his first-grade class memorable. To me, bread was status.

We visited Adi-Hayo many times during the summer of 1982, sometimes staying there for weeks. This time, though, our vocabulary was completely changed. We were fully urbanized. We had become visitors to Adi-Hayo. Thankfully, the people in Adi-Hayo never treated us any differently. We still were their nephews, nieces, and cousins.

My parents felt confident that our life in the city was sustainable, and my mom brought my oldest brother, Afewerki, and my younger sisters Simret and Akberet from Adi-Hayo to join us in Asmara before summer ended, in time for Afewerki and Simret to get registered for school in September. Because of his age and his previous school record, Afewerki started fourth grade at Fre-Selam Elementary School. Simret started kindergarten at Amanuel Public Elementary School, and little Akberet was still at home.

My uncle Yohanes, my mom's younger brother, also came from Adi-Tsenaf and started living with us in Asmara. Yohanes was working at the Ethiopian Electricity and Light Authority.

Back left to right: Uncles Yohanes and Afewerki;
front left to right: Akberet, me, and Simret

By the fall of 1982, my mom and my aunt were supporting me, my brother, Afewerki, my sisters Lemlem, Rutha, Simret, and Akberet, my uncle Yohanes, my grandmother Letensie, and my great-grandmother Itay Nigisa. In addition to our relatives who frequently stayed with us when they came to Asmara for shopping or to bring us barley, wheat, and other farm products from Adi-Hayo, there were eleven of us living in two regular rooms and two half-size rooms.

Mom put Afewerki into an internship at Aboy Dolci's auto shop. Afewerki went to school in the mornings and worked at Aboy Dolci's garage in the afternoons. Thanks to my mom's wisdom, my brother was eventually able to become a successful auto mechanic in the United States. In 2016, as this account is being written, Afewerki owns a well-known auto repair shop—AK Motors—in the Washington, DC, suburb of Silver Spring, Maryland.

One Saturday afternoon at the beginning of my second-grade year, in September 1982, the owner of the carpentry shop called me and the other apprentices into his office. Once we got to the office, the boss said, *"Piccolo"*—the generic name he called us all—"you don't have to come back to work next week. I am giving you vacation for the rest of your life." At the beginning we did not understand what the boss meant by that. But once we told our friends, we became the laughingstocks of our neighborhood for the entire weekend. It became apparent that we'd been dismissed and our apprenticeships terminated.

Mom then had me start a Bible study in the afternoons at St. George Orthodox Church. She felt I had gotten sufficient training in carpentry, and she considered the five dollars a week I was making to be more than I could handle. Five dollars was the monthly rent each of the families who lived in our house paid, while I was making the huge sum of twenty dollars per month. To my mom, this was too much money for a second grader to handle responsibly. Besides, almost all of the neighborhood kids who were believers of the Christian Orthodox faith went to the Bible study at St. George Orthodox Church.

At the church, we studied አ በ ገ ዳ (a bu gi da, an arrangement of the Geez alphabet that is different than the standard academic arrangement). These seemingly disorganized Geez letters are arranged in what seem to be random patterns. But, if close attention is paid, unique patterns appear—even though none of us kids could see at the time. Most of the teachings in the church were learned through rote memorization. Our teachers gave us books to read and memorize. Considering our reading speed in second grade, and the fact that we had little prior knowledge of the Geez language, it was difficult to recite the prayers and the different passages at the speed required by our teachers and headmaster Aboy Yenieta. (Aboy Yenieta is loosely translated as Father Lord, as *aboy* means father and *Yenieta* is an expression derived from two Amharic terms, *yenie gieta*, for "my lord.")

When our teachers believed we were ready to pass to the next level, they sent us to Father Yenieta for approval. Father Yenieta was blind, but his exceptional ears caught every mistake we made in either pronunciation or tone. He was trained not to read but to commit to memory. We all had to make sure we were more than prepared before we faced Father Yenieta—or we knew we would get any number of hard taps on our heads. When we went to see Father Yenieta to test us, he would have us sit next to him and would hold us tightly by one arm so we could not wiggle away. He would tell us when to start our recitations and would tap us hard on our heads to correct us if we made any mistakes. By the end of the year, in addition to some of the Psalms, most of us had committed to memory the Lord's Prayer, the Nicene Creed, and the Hail Mary (Angelic Salutation), in the ancient language of Geez.

After observing the progress I had made in Bible study, Father Habtemichael, our village priest, suggested to my mom that I be inducted into deaconship. According to his proposal, I would ultimately become a priest. With training in the priesthood, coupled with my academic training according to my uncle's vision, by the time I completed high school I could easily become a leader in any church of my choice. But, knowing enough about the stringent rules and regulations of the church, I declined the offer, and Mom supported me. That refusal terminated my Bible study at St. George Orthodox Church.

Unfortunately, not everything in Asmara turned out for the best. The Ethiopian military was still enforcing a strict curfew, and life grew steadily harder and harder for my friends and family.

During the second week of November 1982, Mom and Lemlem went to Adi-Hayo to prepare for the celebration of St. Mary, the most significant annual holiday celebrated in the village. A week after Mom and Lemlem left, the day before the holiday, my younger sisters Rutha and Simret, Aunt Ezgharia, and I got ready to take a bus to join Mom and the rest of our family. We boarded the bus heading toward the southern region of the country at the downtown bus station. Simret and I sat on the right side and Rutha and Aunt Ezgharia sat across from us on the left side.

The bus started moving, and we passed the checkpoint at the end of the city in a short while. Not long after we passed the second checkpoint in a place called Sela'e-da'ero, the bus started moving faster than before. Too fast. Nervously, some people inside the bus started trying to grab whatever was near them. Others started shouting at the driver and getting up from their seats. When some saw that we would crash, they tried to jump out the door while the bus was still moving.

Dust covered me in an instant, and then I was outside. I either blacked out or I have lost my memory, because all I remember is standing in front of my younger sister Rutha, who was lying down on the road with her eyes open. I looked toward the mountain and saw our bus upside down. Women were crying with their hands on their heads. Men were moving back and forth with their lips moving, but I could not hear what they were saying. Finally, an elderly lady came and grabbed me away from where my sister was lying. She asked me if I knew the kid lying down, and I told her she was my sister. She then held me closer and hugged me, covering my face with her clothing. A few minutes later, I saw my sister Simret across from me, and I called her name. She came, and the lady held Simret's hand from one side and me from the other side. The lady then asked me if I knew where I lived, and I told her I did.

As I was told later, we crashed because the brakes failed to stop the bus as we were going down the mountain. Rutha had held onto the jacket of a man who was trying to jump out of the bus. After he jumped, Rutha fell on her head, and she was critically injured. Even though Rutha was driven to the hospital in Asmara, she was pronounced dead upon arrival.

My dad came from Saudi Arabia for Rutha's burial. It was the most disheartening experience for him. He left his home in order to support his family, and yet he lost one of his younger children before he got a chance to see her a second time.

For me the burial was a different experience. The image of Rutha that I saw when she was lying down on the road remained on my mind for many years. But most importantly, seeing my dad gave me a chance to put a concrete face on my father. I had no memory of him before that time. I was too young to remember his face before he left Eritrea.

During that difficult year, I took on yet another job: I became a regular letter writer for my family members and the elders from the village whose children were scattered abroad in the diaspora. Looking back, I believe writing letters for my elders made me grow up much faster than my peers. In every letter I wrote, I learned new idioms, adages, and proverbs. The village elders had a way of expressing their feelings using imagery. A typical paragraph, one you would find in nearly every letter I wrote for an elder, would be:

ናብ ዝኸበርኪን ዝተናፈቕኪን ምሕረት ጓለይ፡፡ ኣቐዳመ ዝኸበረን
ዝዓዘዘን ሰላምታይ የቐርበልኪ፡፡ ከመይ ትኾኒ ኣለኺ. ጸጋ ጥዕናኺ፡፡
ንሕና ኣብዚ ዘለና ብሙሉኣትና እንትርፊ ናትኪ ናፍቖት እንተዘይኮይኑ
ኣዝግኣብሄር ይመስገን ብጣዕሚ ጽቡቕ ኣለና፡፡ ንስኺዉን ከምቲ
ንሕና ጽቡቕ ዘለና'ዮ ጽቡቕ ንኽትህልዊ ሰብ ሙሉኣት ተስፋ
ኢና፡፡ እነሃት እዛ ደብዳቤይ ከም መርከብ ባሕሪ ስጊራ: ከም ዑፍ
በሪራ: ነቦን ሩባን ተሳጊራ ናፍቖት ሓዘል ሰላምታይ ከተብጽሓልኪ
ይልእኸልኪ ኣለኹ፡፡

To my daughter Mehret, whom I miss dearly; first, I
would like to extend my regards and best wishes. How
are you doing? Thanks to God, those of us who are here
are doing fine. We also wish and hope you are doing fine
as well. I am sending my letter hoping it sails through
the sea like a ship and soars through the mountains and
valleys like a bird to deliver my heartfelt longing for you.

Writing letters for the elders truly made me appreciate the
depth and wealth of my mother tongue, and of a culture that
was to sustain me through my exile years. It instilled, at a very
young age, a pride and unshakable self-identity that I would
need through the long voyage I had to travel in life. In fact,
during my years in Kenya and the United States, I became an
ardent reader of Tigrinya books and listener of Eritrean music, thanks to the strong sense of identity I acquired during
this letter-writing period.

In 1983, I went to Amanuel Elementary School's branch
in Gejeret in the mornings for third grade. We used to call

that branch of Amanuel "Enda Nora"—the lime place. The neighborhood was named after a factory that manufactured lime to be used in cement. Iyoba and I would get to school at six a.m. and play *salvati* with the rest of our schoolmates until the school bell rang at seven a.m. Salvati is a game similar to the American game of tag, but played in teams. Since I had ended both my apprenticeship at the carpentry shop and religious study at St. George Orthodox Church by the end of second grade, during the next two years I had a lot of time to play soccer and other games with my friends after school and during the weekends.

We played soccer in tournaments organized by Samuel Tedros Gebru, a young man who was a godsend to our neighborhood. While he attended middle school at the Colegio La Salle Catholic School, he organized soccer tournaments for us during the summer (the rainy season in that part of the world) and cross-country track races during the winter (the hot season). Samuel also participated in tournaments that he organized for his own age group. For every tournament, Samuel made sure we had enough money for trophies and soccer shirts. This was done through collective fund-raising, by going throughout the city soliciting financial assistance while displaying our respective teams' jerseys. Some of us also got money from our parents.

Overall, our living situation was on par with if not better than most of our neighbors. For all practical purposes, we were one of the few "home owners" in the area. Mom was the de facto landlord, representing Aunt Abrehet, and all the renters in our compound treated my mom accordingly. Thanks to Aunt Abrehet, we didn't have to go through the agony and endless torment of rental housing. My family did not have to go through the monthly fiasco of bickering with landlords about water, electricity, and other bills that were shared among the renters within a given compound.

Financially, my dad made sure we lived comfortably by sending us money from Saudi Arabia, where he worked as a truck driver. Life for immigrants in Saudi Arabia was miserable and despondent—they couldn't, and cannot to this day, own property or even open a bank account. My dad and other immigrants were required to pay a significant portion of their income annually to someone who would "sponsor" them to live there. My dad, working hard to support us, was sharing a room with other Eritrean immigrants while his children were earning such bourgeoisie nicknames as "children of Jeddah," because we were living off money sent from the capital of Saudi Arabia.

Whenever Aunt Abrehet or my dad came home, we were treated with new clothes, school accessories, and of course candies that we used to make friends in our neighborhood.

The candy bars we were getting from Jeddah were unlike the animal crackers produced and distributed locally by the Asmara Biscuit Factory. The gifts became our exit and entry visas simultaneously: exit visa from the village kids' moniker and entry visa to the highly esteemed and exclusive Asmarino club. The label "Asmarino" was solely for the city kids who considered themselves to be culturally advanced, highly sophisticated, and all-knowing. It just was not conceivable for any kid in the various neighborhoods of Asmara not to seek membership to this elite and highly esteemed club.

During one of his trips to Asmara, my dad brought a lot of suitcases. When we saw the suitcases getting unloaded from

47

the cars outside our house, we were so excited we could not wait to see what was inside. It seemed as if he had emptied all the stores in Jeddah to bring us the clothing, toys, and candies in those suitcases. But a day or two later, strangers started taking the suitcases one at a time, and we did not know what to say. We were really angry and upset when all the suitcases were gone. We did not hide our anger from our dad, and we asked him how he could have done that to us. My dad called me, my sisters, and my brother and gathered us in the room. He then told us that other Eritreans working in Saudi Arabia had asked him to bring gifts to their families in Asmara. At the airport, he'd had too many suitcases, and when the airline personnel told him he would not be able to take them all, he decided to leave his behind and bring the rest with him. He told us he'd brought other people's items and left ours behind because the families that were picking up those suitcases were deprived of enjoying their fathers' and/or mothers' presence, and they should at least be able to enjoy their gifts. He said we had our father with us to spend the holiday and that should mean everything to us.

At the time, we were not really convinced of his rationale. We just shrugged our shoulders. After a while, though, my dad's instinctive decision became one of the most precious life lessons he ever taught me.

Starting in 1983, obligatory military service was instituted by the Ethiopian government for males above eighteen years of age. In practice, though, weight was used as an enlistment qualification. Any young boy weighing forty-five kilograms (one hundred pounds) or more was found to be eligible and sent to the front line after six months of military training. Each district in Asmara and each village in Eritrea, based on population, was assigned quotas of conscripts. To avoid the forced military conscription enforced by the Ethiopian government, Eritrean youngsters joined the Eritrean People's Liberation Front in large flocks. Those who stayed behind, like my brother, Afewerki, started spending the nights away from home during the enlistment period, which was twice a year for about a month.

During the 1984 famine, the Ethiopian government also started employing food aid as a means of recruitment. Based on the number of family members enlisted in the Ethiopian army, each family was given a certain amount of grain and food oil from the aid that was provided to the Ethiopian government to combat the famine. Food aid was withheld from a number of Eritrean villages because they did not fulfill their quotas of conscripts.

My uncle Yohanes was able to avoid the conscription by maintaining his address in Adi-Tsenaf while living with us in Asmara. At times, he also stayed at other family members' houses when rumors about house-to-house searches started going around our neighborhood. House-to-house searches usually focused around specific neighborhoods at a time, and information frequently leaked through the neighborhood rumor mills.

My brother, Afewerki, received a draft letter from our Kebelle, the neighborhood or zonal administrative unit, which required him to report and be weighed. Forty-five kilograms was the cutoff weight for military service, and Afewerki was over the cutoff. With the help of Uncle Yohanes, who was able to maneuver the system by bribing the Ethiopian officials, Afewerki's weight was found to be forty-two kilograms, giving him a pass for that round of conscription.

Afewerki also managed to dodge the house-to-house searches looking for recruits by spending the nights at various relatives' houses in Asmara. Finally, in May 1985, Afewerki went to Addis Ababa to avoid conscription completely and stayed there with the family of Aya Mohammed Kelifa Adem Hasebu of Adi-Hayo.[10] With the help of my dad in Saudi Arabia and Aya Mohammed in Addis Ababa, Afewerki was able to go to Egypt in June 1985 and apply for political asylum. My youngest sister, Tigisti, was born on July 4, 1986, a year after Afewerki left home.

---

10 *Aya* is a respectful term for an older brother or close family member.

AS GOLD IS TESTED BY FIRE

"Whatsoever is brought upon thee take cheerfully,
and be patient when thou art changed to a low
estate. For gold is tried in the fire, and acceptable
men in the furnace of adversity."
—Ecclesiasticus 2:4–5

Eritrea is located along the western coast of the Red Sea, south of Egypt and the Sudan, and north of Ethiopia and Djibouti. The region is usually referred to as the Horn of Africa.

The genesis of modern Eritrea reads like the script of all modern African countries: European missionaries survey a land, seize property, and pass it to their governments, and overnight a group of people already inhabiting the land are declared subjects and obligated to submit. Mzee Jomo Kenyatta, Kenya's first president, is credited with the following widely known statement: "When the missionaries arrived, the Africans had the land and the missionaries had the Bible. They taught us how to pray with our eyes closed. When we opened them, they had the land and we had the Bible."

Before and during the arrival of the Italians in the late nineteenth century, the inhabitants of present-day Eritrea were going through acute famine and drought and continuous warfare with invaders coming from Egypt to the north and Shoa and Tigray warlords coming from the south—parts of present-day Ethiopia.

The British traveler Augustus B. Wylde presented very detailed and vivid accounts of the famine, drought, cholera, and wars that had devastated Eritrea and the surrounding region. The following is one of the many horrific details from Adi-Qeyh, a town in the southern part of Eritrea, Wylde recounted:[11]

> "From a distance a hamlet on the mountain side might be seen, and looked as if it were perfect, only no people could be seen moving about, and no smoke issuing from the cottages. On approaching, the roofs of the huts would be found in bad repair, and on entering it, not a human being was to be seen. The doors of the building were nearly off their hinges, the thornbushes that shut the enclosures round the huts were to one side, and grass and weeds were growing everywhere; a more luxurious patch of vegetation or rank grass, about six feet length by two in breath, would mark the spot where some poor victim lay unburied. On looking into the houses they would be found as if the occupants had just vacated them, but on closer examination, when the eye got accustomed to the semi-darkness inside after the glare of the bright sunshine in the open, several skeletons would be found, either

11 Wylde, Augustus B., *Modern Abyssinia*. London: Methuen & Co., 1901.

on the raised end of the hut or on a bedstead. In one hut I found five remains; one was that of a woman, as I could tell by the remains of her dress, alongside of her on the same bed lay two small skeletons, one a little larger than the other, both of the little skulls resting on the arm bones of what perhaps was their mother. Behind the door was another body, evidently a boy, the leg bones stretched out and those of the upper part of the body in a small heap. The owner of them had evidently died with his back resting against the wall; the last body was curled up near the fireplace alongside which were several empty cooking vessels. One examination of these abandoned villages was enough for me, and from this specimen I could see what this fertile country had suffered from the series of years of war, famine, and pestilence."

Wylde reported the destruction of many villages he found on his way. In addition to the acute famine and drought of unprecedented proportions of the second half of the late 1800s, and the cholera, typhus, and smallpox epidemics in 1889, present-day Eritrea had become a battlefield of competing invaders: the likes of Egypt and Italy, expansionists such as the Mahdists coming from Sudan, and the rulers of Tigray and Shoa coming from the northern part of present-day Ethiopia. The battles of Gundet, Gura'e, Kufit, and Dogali were but a few of the battles fought within the borders of present-day Eritrea.[12]

---

12 According to Zemihret Yohanes's book *Resistance Against Italian Colonialism in Eritrea,* written in Tigrinya. The battles of Gundet and Gura'e were fought between Abyssinian emperor Yohannes IV and the Egyptians in October 1875 and March 1876, respectively. The battle of Kufit was fought between Alula Aba Nega and the Mahdist army in September 1885.

At the same time, Alula Aba Nega, representing Emperor Yohannes IV of Tigray, was in a constant battle with Ra'esi Woldemichael Solomon,[13] ruling the inhabitants of the major parts of Eritrea with the town of Debarwa as its capital.

Alula finally realized that he wouldn't be able to defeat Ra'esi Woldemichael Solomon while fighting the Mahdis and the Egyptians on multiple fronts. Alula declared a truce in 1879, and Ra'esi Woldemichael accepted the call for peace. Alula invited Ra'esi Woldemichael to attend a ceremony to sign a peace treaty with Emperor Yohannes IV and made a solemn oath by swearing on the Bible, guaranteeing Ra'esi Woldemichael's safe return after signing the agreement. Ra'esi Woldemichael went to sign the treaty and, to his dismay, found himself surrounded by Alula Aba Nega's army. This ended the reign of Bahri Negus once and for all and opened the gate for further expansion of the Tigray warlord Emperor Yohannes IV.

In January 1887, the Italians were devastated and embarrassed by their loss at the battle of Dogali at the hands of Ras Alula, the great Ethiopian general. The publicity of the defeat with the details of the massacre of European soldiers added an insult to the already painful defeat.

Italy wanted to avenge its loss. Emperor Yohannes IV wanted to expand his sphere of influence. Present-day Eritrea became the battlefield of the invading Italian army and Emperor Yohannes IV's expansionist dream. The inhabitants of the area continued to become victims of outsiders.

On May 2, 1889, King Menelik of Shoa, the rival and successor of Emperor Yohannes IV, and the Italians signed the

13 The crown prince successor of Bahri Negus (King of the Sea), the king of Medri Bahri ("Land of the Sea" in the Tigrinya language).

Wuchalie treaty, defining the borders between the northern part of modern-day Ethiopia and what was to become the Italian colony of Eritrea. Menelik recognized Eritrea as an Italian colony, while the Italians reciprocated the deal by recognizing Menelik as the sole ruler of Shoa.

In 1890, Eritrea was formally declared an Italian colony. Multiple treaties were signed with the British (who were in the Sudan), the French (who were in Djibouti), and an Abyssinian king, Menelik II, defining the borders between Eritrea and Ethiopia as we know them today.

Italian colonization of Eritrea was not without obstacles. The Italians were getting fierce resistance from the lords of the central and southern fiefdoms, emirs of the western and the Red Sea sultanates, and community leaders of the various nationalities that make up Eritrea. The Italians were aggressively suppressing the comparably lightly armed Eritrean resistance forces. The Italians started detaining Eritrean community leaders in Nakura Island in the Red Sea, which became the Italian version of the infamous US federal prison of Alcatraz.

If we are to accept the definition of a society—a group of people with shared experiences and common destiny—then Eritreans commenced their resistance as a people of a modern-day nation-state in Nakura Island. The nobles of modern-day Eritrea, the lords of the various fiefdoms, the emirs, and the community leaders who were imprisoned there started planning what is known among Eritreans and Italians as "the great escape." The Italian colonizers' wishes and dreams were to bury Eritrean identity and nationalism underneath Nakura Island and to make sure future generations "know only the names of those who have made Italy great."[14] To the contrary, Nakura Island became the incubator of Eritrean nationalism and national identity.

Nakura Island is located in the Dahlak Archipelago, situated about fifty kilometers (thirty-one miles) east of the port city of Massawa. By the end of 1899, there were about 119 Eritrean community leaders and notables detained in Nakura, guarded by twenty-seven Eritrean Ascari troops led by two Italian commanders. On November 12, 1899, twelve prisoners who were taken to fetch water from one of the wells overtook the six Ascari guarding them and killed one of the two Italian commanders. During the confrontation that followed, the prisoners killed some and captured the remaining Ascari and the second Italian commander. They eventually took full control of the island and freed the remaining 107 prisoners. Led by the "breaker of Nakura" Ali Mohammed Osman Buri, the prisoners left Nakura Island. Most of the them successfully reached the mainland and continued their resistance against the Italian occupation by crossing to the northern part of Ethiopia. Some of them unfortunately died en route to freedom.

Once Eritreans were able to break the barriers of Nakura prison, the proverbial Pandora's box was opened once and for all. Future colonizers and "administrators" and "trustees" of Eritrea were haunted by the successive generations of Eritreans, who continued the struggle for independence. The

---

14 Trevaskis, G. K. N. *Eritrea: A Colony in Transition: 1941-52.* London: Oxford University Press, 1960.

forefathers of modern-day Eritrea considered Eritrean identity and nationalism as one of the necessary criteria for selecting people to join them to rise up against colonizers.[15]

Most of the "breakers of Nakura" went to the northern part of modern-day Ethiopia and continued their resistance and opposition to Italian occupation. The Italian colonizers raised their concern about the armed resistance Eritrean notables were waging from the northern part of Ethiopia to King Menelik. Italy agreed to recognize Menelik as the sole ruler of modern-day Ethiopia, while Menelik reciprocated by recognizing Eritrea as an Italian colony. As a sign of his newly found friendship with the Europeans, Menelik also agreed to sever his ties with the Eritrean resistance that had made it difficult for the Italians to rule Eritrea. True to his promise, Menelik captured and detained most of the Eritrean nobles and community leaders who were waging armed resistance from their bases in the northern part of Ethiopia, paving the way for Italian expansion with limited opposition from within Eritrea. Menelik was unaware of Italy's plan to consolidate its power and use Eritrea as a launching pad for further expansion. Eventually, in 1935, Italy under Benito Mussolini invaded Ethiopia and ruled the country until 1941.

15   In his Tigrinya book titled *Eritrea's Heroic Ancestors and Our Culture,* Yishak Yosief presents the following as the three main reasons the Eritrean compatriots at Nakura prison decided to approach Ali Mohammed Osman Buri (referred in the Afar language as *Nakura yagali*, which literally means "breaker of Nakura") to join them for the great escape:

1. As an Eritrean, they could count on his nationalistic tendencies.

2. Since Mohammed Ali Osman Buri's father was in the boat rental business, the Italians could have rented some of his family's boats.

3. Since Mohammed Ali Osman Buri was well acquainted with the people sailing the boats, he could easily obtain their trust.

The Italian colonization in Eritrea lasted until the middle of World War II. In 1941, the Italians were finally ejected from Eritrea by the Allied powers, led by the British. But at the end of the war, one of the early acts of the newly formed United Nations was to deny Eritreans their right to self-determination. Eritrea was initially left under the custody of the British military administration. A decade later, Eritrea was federated with Ethiopia. The federation with Ethiopia was supposed to last for ten years, and then Eritreans would be able to decide their future through referendum. Instead, the Ethiopian feudal rulers unilaterally dissolved the federation and nullified the Eritrean parliament.

The human aspect of history can usually get lost or overshadowed by political history. While the genesis of modern Eritrea was like the rest of Africa, what makes the Eritrean case unique is the fact that Eritreans endured a brutal oppression and colonization by a fellow African neighbor. Out of the fifty-three former European colonies in Africa, Eritrea was the only country to be denied independence after its European masters departed.

Each of Eritrea's colonizers applied its own system of oppression to subdue and dehumanize the population: Italian apartheid used segregation; British rule was marked by a divide-and-rule strategy; while Ethiopian rulers were determined to "dry the sea to kill the fish." All of them aimed to subdue Eritreans and kill the people's aspirations to be independent.

The Italians used both segregation and limited access to formal education as a means of sustaining their system of apartheid. "The denial of education—or the use of education or instruction for repressive indoctrination or manipulation—is a significant means of restricting liberty and curbing access to power," Theodore Cross wrote in *The Black Power Imperative*.[16] During the Italian colonization, fourth grade was the highest level of Italian language–based formal education a native Eritrean could acquire. "By the end of his fourth year, the Eritrean student should be able to speak our language moderately well; he should know the four arithmetical operations within normal limits… and of history he should know only the names of those who have made Italy great."[17]

The downtown areas of the capital city, Asmara, and the port city of Massawa were designated as "whites only." Additionally, a number of whites-only military camps were scattered across the nation. The only two groups of nonwhite native Eritreans that had access to these parts were maids and interpreters. While many of the Italian men saw no contradiction in sleeping with African women and producing mixed-race children, none saw fit to legalize their unions with Africans.

British rule did not last long—Eritrea was under the British military administration for only ten years. But the damage the British inflicted on Eritrea in that short period is no less significant than that of either their predecessors or their successors. As victors in World War II, the British took it

16   Cross, Theodore. *The Black Power Imperative: Racial Inequality and the Politics of Nonviolence.* New York: Faulkner, 1987.

17   Trevaskis, *G. K. N. Eritrea: A Colony in Transition: 1941–52.* London: Oxford University Press, 1960.

upon themselves to rob Eritrea of everything they considered valuable: from floating dry docks to whole factories; from oil-drilling machinery to railway cars. All of it was shamelessly sold in the open. In a few years, they deprived Eritrea of what in today's currency would amount to nearly half a billion dollars. The aim of it all was to prove that Eritrea was not economically viable and thus either the British themselves or one of their allies should rule the land, or at least part of it, as Stephen H. Longrigg wrote in *A Short History of Eritrea*: "The single Eritrea of today is doomed. Dismemberment, in some form and to some extent, must be the alternative."[18]

To give their scheme an international face, they tried to sell the idea of partitioning Eritrea in their Bevin-Sforza Plan. The Bevin-Sforza Plan was drafted by Ernest Bevin and Count Carlo Sforza (the British foreign secretary and Italian foreign minister at the time) to decide the fate of the Libyans, Eritreans, and Somalis that were under Italian colonization. Under the Bevin-Sforza plan, first, Libya was to become a trusteeship of the United Nations, while Britain, France, and Italy would continue to administer its three provinces for ten years, after which Libya would become independent. Second, Somalia was to be placed under Italian trusteeship for however long the United Nations General Assembly decided. And third, Eritrea was to be split into two parts: the Highland Christians to join Ethiopia and the Lowland Muslims to join the British colony in the Sudan. The reaction of Muslim and Christian Eritreans to this plan was swift: we survive

---

18   Longrigg, Stephen H. *A Short History of Eritrea*. Oxford: Clarendon Press, 1945. This is the same Longrigg who was writing in the newspapers published in Eritrea using an Eritrean pen name.

or perish as one people. The plan was rejected at the United Nations General Assembly on May 18, 1949. The British and Americans then went to their plan B—obstructing and frustrating Eritrea's aspiration for independence by placing it under feudal Ethiopia in a federal arrangement.

On February 13, 1945, Emperor Haile Selassie of Ethiopia was flown to Deversoir Air Base in Egypt to meet US president Franklin Delano Roosevelt and discuss "Ethiopia's need for a port. In reply to the president's question as to whether this should be Djibouti or Eritrea, the emperor said that from a short-term point of view Djibouti would be the best port because of the existing railway, but that a long-term policy required a port in Eritrea. The president inquired regarding the possibility of building a railway to such a port and was told it could be done; he advised that in case this was undertaken by an American company, too much should not be paid for its services, and added that he would give the same advice in regard to the petroleum in case that matter should ever come up."[19]

The understanding between Haile Selassie and FDR was fully supported by Harry Truman's administration. The US Joint Chiefs of Staff submitted a memorandum to James Forrestal, secretary of defense under President Harry Truman's administration, stating, "As to the nature of the

19 *Foreign Relations of the United States*, 1945, Volume VIII, eds. Rogers P. Churchill, Laurence Evans, Herbert A. Fine, John P. Glennon, and Ralph R. Goodwin (Washington, Government Printing Office, 1969), Documents 1–6.

rights in Eritrea, the Joint Chiefs of Staff would state categorically that the benefits now resulting from operation of our telecommunications center at Asmara—benefits common and of high military importance to both the United States and Great Britain—can be obtained from no other location in the entire Middle East–Eastern Mediterranean area. Therefore, United States rights in Eritrea should not be compromised."[20]

The basis and rationale for US interest in Eritrea can easily be summarized by a letter to Secretary of State James F. Byrnes. The letter from Sinclair Oil Corporation, headquartered at 630 Fifth Avenue in New York City, dated September 27, 1945, reads as follows:

> The Honorable James F. Byrnes
> Secretary of State
> Washington, DC
>
> Dear Mr. Secretary:
>
> My company has only recently completed an agreement with the Imperial Ethiopian government for the development of petroleum in Ethiopia.
>
> I feel rather certain that you, personally, have been informed with respect to this agreement. Unfortunately, the country of Ethiopia is an inland country, with no direct water outlet for export shipping. Should we be successful in discovering oil, we would, of necessity, be required to construct adequate pipeline facil-

---

20 *Foreign Relations of the United States*, 1948, Volume III, eds. Frederick Aandahl, Ralph R. Goodwin, Marvin W. Kranz, Charles S. Sampson, Howard McGaw Smyth, and David H. Stauffer (Washington, Government Printing Office, 1974), Document 587.

ities from Ethiopia to a suitable seaport, as well as an export shipping terminal. If we are to proceed with our development program in Ethiopia, it is of vital importance that Eritrea should be recognized as an integral part of Ethiopia, as we would have a suitable seaport outlet.

Our entire development program will seriously be delayed and affected should Eritrea be under the domination of any other power except Ethiopia. I, therefore, urgently request that your good offices support the demands of Ethiopia with respect to Eritrea.

For your personal information, I am attaching hereto photostatic copy of the supplemental agreement between my company and the Imperial Ethiopian government, with respect to construction of pipelines in outboard outlets, from which you will readily see the importance to this project of the acquisition of Eritrea by Ethiopia.

Very truly yours,

Signed:
H. F. Sinclair
President[21]

There are few countries in Africa and the third world that can rival the attention that Ethiopia received from Europe and the United States. This attention did not happen overnight. It took many decades. Most of it was accidental, and

---

21 "The Role of Sinclair Oil Corporation in the Ethio-Eritrean Federation." *Journal of Eritrean Studies*. Volume 4, No. 1-2. Summer/Winter 1989. p. 73-76.

the rest was deliberate propaganda from the monarchs and the European Ethiophiles.

There are a number of factors that may have contributed to this interest. For a long time, Europeans were looking for the land of Prester John, the legendary wealthy Christian patriarch and king who defied expansion of Islam. Portuguese explorers who visited Abyssinia in the 1500s claimed that this was the "Christian island surrounded by sea of Islam" defended by King Prester John. This myth of the "Christian island" set the narrative of history, and the Coptic Orthodox Church, the monarchy, the Amhara people and culture became a center of attention of European travelers, scholars, and writers.

King Menelik I, who ruled Abyssinia around 950 BC, is believed to be the son of King Solomon of ancient Israel and Makeda, ancient Queen of Sheba. The story of Sheba added to the myth of Ethiopian uniqueness. The monarchy's claim to have descended from King Solomon, conquering lion of the tribe of Judah, was greatly exploited by successive Abyssinian monarchs in order to sustain their claim to the throne and to create a strong alliance with the Europeans.

Unfortunately, this myth-cum-reality of the Solomonic emperor of Ethiopia is difficult for many Ethiopians and Ethiophiles to grow out of. The historical fiction of King Menelik I—which could easily pass for a chapter in one of the Greek mythologies—is blindly accepted and presented by present-day Ethiopians as a historical fact. The presence of Ethiopian Jews, now accepted in Israel as the "lost tribe," also adds to the fascination.

Foreign advisers, such as John Hathaway Spencer from the US, guided and helped Ethiopia to get attention from the Western media and favorable treatment by the Western nations. Guilt for not having helped Emperor Haile Selassie at the League of Nations was translated into direct help for the country after the war, be it in letting him have Eritrea or favorable treatment in international politics and economic aid. The emperor played his hand well in siding with the West in the Cold War—sending troops on the UN side to Korea, Congo, and other trouble spots.

Without giving any consideration to the wishes and aspirations of Eritreans, "Eritrea was federated with Ethiopia in 1952 not because of the proofs of history but because the Ethiopian version fitted the interests of the foreign powers which decided the future of Eritrea after the defeat of Italy in the Second World War."[22]

To see the absurdity and incompatibility of the federal arrangement made between Ethiopia and Eritrea, all one has to do is compare Article 4 of the Ethiopian Constitution as revised in 1955 and Articles 17 and 18 of the Eritrean Constitution. The Ethiopian version states, "Due to his lineage from the Solomonic dynasty, and being chosen by God, the emperor is a holy man. His honor is not to be violated. His power is not to be questioned… He who attempts to hurt the emperor will be punished."[23]

22   Pool, David. *Eritrea: Africa's Longest War.* London: Anti-Slavery Society, 1982. p. 8.

23   People's Front for Democracy and Justice, *History of Eritrea: From Ancient Times to Independence,* May 2015.

The Eritrean versions of Articles 17 and 18 state, "The Eritrean Constitution is based on the democratic principle of a government... All government officials are elected from within the general public... They are elected through free and fair voting processes. They work to serve the people."[24]

The British and the Americans provided the Ethiopian feudal lords with the political and institutional cover to grab more land than they had administered during the preceding centuries. These warlords, left to their own ambitions, would have been happy to live south of the Mereb River, the physical border between Eritrea and Ethiopia as negotiated by King Menelik II of Shoa and the Italian colonizers of Eritrea.

Under the protection and full political and institutional cover of the British, and with the American John Hathaway Spencer directing Ethiopia's foreign policy, in 1962 the Ethiopian feudal lords nullified the United Nations federal agreement and declared Eritrea the fourteenth province of Ethiopia.

A year before Ethiopia annexed Eritrea, sensing Ethiopia's ultimate desire, Eritreans gave up on getting justice through peaceful means and began their armed struggle for independence. On September 1, 1961, a group of Eritreans from various parts of the country, and some from the diaspora, launched the military struggle to uproot Ethiopian colonialism.

As gold is tested by fire, Eritreans were tested time and again for their fortitude. Their slogan, "our struggle is long and bitter but victory is certain," spread throughout Eritrea. It was the slogan of innocent people entangled in a situation completely outside their control.

---

24 People's Front for Democracy and Justice, *History of Eritrea: From Ancient Times to Independence*, May 2015.

TEACH A KID TO FISH...

"Books were my pass to personal freedom. I
learned to read at age three and soon discovered
there was a whole world to conquer that went
beyond our farm in Mississippi." —Oprah Winfrey

In 1986, I was registered for fifth grade at my regular
day school, Amanuel Elementary School, during the afternoon, and sixth grade in the evening shift at Comboni
Elementary and Middle School. Lemlem was also going to
Comboni in the evening to take an additional course that
could prepare her for the eighth-grade national examination. Regardless of how well one does in school, a student
cannot pass to middle school or continue on to high school
unless the student passes the national examinations given at
the end of sixth and eighth grades.

Lemlem and I—more her than me, mostly—were getting
some challenges on our way to school. In one incident, we'd
walked for about two and half blocks from our house and
turned left at the corner of Colegio La Salle. This guy came
out of nowhere and grabbed Lemlem by her shoulder. Lemlem
was startled and tried to curse him off. I jumped in the middle
and started cursing at him. The guy could easily have pushed

me off, but instead he pulled a gun out of his jacket. Lemlem and I looked at each other and decided to run as fast as we could. I ran for few minutes while continuously glancing over my shoulder. I finally stopped when I was sure the guy had not followed me.

I was not sure whether the guy followed Lemlem or not. I did not see to what direction Lemlem ran. I was not even sure if she had actually run away. I just assumed she had because that was what I did. By the time I stopped, I realized I was in the Alfa-Romeo neighborhood, a block away from Amanuel Elementary School. To avoid any possibility of encountering the guy again, I avoided going back home through Colegio La Salle. Instead, I went by Radio Marina, the Italian naval radio station that later became a US military base and is now an Ethiopian military base. After roaming around the neighborhood and making sure I was not followed, I went home and found Lemlem sitting next to my mom, worried to death about my whereabouts. Lemlem apparently had run toward San Francisco Catholic Church, which was a couple of blocks away from our house, and then gone straight home.

We had more unpleasant encounters with kids known to most of us Eritreans as "the kids from Kagnew," because they lived with their Ethiopian parents at the military barracks inside Kagnew Station. Considering the close proximity of Cambo Bolo to Kagnew Station, Lemlem and I were actually passing through their territories on our way to school. But we had to go to school, and that was the shortest way to get to Comboni.

One day when my dad was visiting, he told us he was going to follow us on the way to school. Lemlem and I left home and took our usual route. After walking for two blocks, we reached the end of Colegio La Salle and turned left at Mereb Street toward Caravel restaurant. We crossed the roundabout and continued heading toward 172-1 Street. Once we finished crossing the roundabout and reached Lateria Senai, across from the Mobil gas station, a kid started roughing us up. My dad came from the back, picked the kid up by his neck, and threw him to the street. The kid, shocked and on the ground looking up at my dad, started talking nonsensically, sometimes apologizing, at times questioning what he did wrong. My dad finally grabbed him by his collar and lifted him off the ground. The kid was still in shock. My dad finally gave a him firm warning and told him he was not to get close to us ever again. The kid kept nodding his head affirmatively, and my dad put him down to his feet.

Lemlem, my dad, and I walked all the way to Comboni Elementary School.

During the second semester, I walked to school alone. On my way to evening classes I would often see a group of neatly dressed boys my age playing soccer. These kids lived only three blocks away from us, but their lives seemed to be much more structured than mine. They were outside at certain hours, but they would always end their games promptly and walk back home together. I was intrigued by their routine. In my household, as long as I was home for lunch at noon and dinner at seven p.m., no one knew or cared where I was for the rest of the day, except, of course, for school.

I decided to get to know these children. One day, I ran up to the ball when one of the boys was getting into position to kick a penalty. I challenged the goalie, offering him a quarter if he successfully blocked my kick. He asked what he would have to do if he missed, and I told him he would not have to give me anything. In fact, I told him, I would use my left foot for the kick. He was excited at the prospect of winning a quarter and prepared himself to defend the goal. I kicked and made a clean goal. He asked me to do it again. I told him I had to go to school, but promised we would play the next day. He did not know I could use both of my feet equally—although I am not ambidextrous, after years of practice I had trained myself to kick a soccer ball with my left foot as strongly and accurately as my right one.

Daniel Mebrahtu Negusse—Dani—the young man I challenged that day, would become my close friend and someone I would admire for many years to come.

I soon learned that Dani, his brother Tsehaye, and his sisters Senait, Rahel, and Aida were allowed to play outside the house for only half an hour in the mornings and half an hour in the afternoons. This puzzled me. I thought being locked inside for most of the day was the cruelest and most unusual punishment I could imagine, yet I was curious to know how they lived and what they did with their time. Dani told me that they read books from the library, played board games, and studied. Studying was the only part I fully understood.

I had never heard of the games he mentioned, nor did I know what a library was. The only games I had mastered till that day were soccer and cards. Dani tried to explain the games to me and told me about the British Council Library.

He invited me to come with him and his siblings the next time they went.

That day I arrived at their house at eight thirty a.m. The British Council Library was located across the street from the American Library, as Dani pointed out when we got there. In one morning, I was going to see two libraries for the first time in my life, and I was excited. The British Council Library opened at ten a.m., and we joined the line that was forming outside and waited for about fifteen minutes before the guard started to let people in, one at a time. When our time came, Dani and Tsehaye showed the guard their two green cards. The guard looked at me. Dani told him that I was with them, but he said I could not get in if I did not have a card. He told me to step aside. Dani begged the guard, but was told, "It is a policy that I cannot violate. He can wait for you right here if he wants." I was furious. I had been looking forward to seeing the inside of a library for the first time. Unfortunately, all I could do that day was try to get a peek from the front door.

While waiting for Dani and his brother to get their books, I asked the guard what the green card was all about and how I could get one. He told me it was a membership card and that, in order to get one, I needed someone who worked for the government to sponsor me. I considered my options, but the only person I could think of was Uncle Yohanes, my maternal uncle who worked as a technician for the Ethiopian Electric Light and Power Authority. I did not think he knew anything about libraries.

Dani and Tsehaye soon came out with their books, and Dani told me how sorry he was. On our way home, I prodded him about how I could get a library card, and he said he would ask their father to sponsor me.

The following Saturday morning, when I stopped by Dani's house, his father, Aboy Mebrahtu Negusse, asked Dani to bring Senait and Rahel's cards. Dani fetched them, and Aboy Mebrahtu gave me the two British Council Library membership cards that opened the door to a world Lemlem and I never knew existed. He said we could use the two cards and exchange books with his kids. He also told me that I was welcome to study with Dani. After that, I went to Dani's house almost daily.

Using Dani's sisters' library cards, I was on my way to conquer the world of books. Before I met Dani Negusse's family, I had only read a few English-language storybooks. But once we got to the British Council Library, I did not know where to start. I was overwhelmed by the sheer volume of books. Rows after rows of books filled the room. My eyes started wandering from one row to another without any idea what I was actually looking at. Finally, I asked Dani to guide me to the right books.

On my first day, he introduced me to the Inspector Thackeray series of children's books by Kenneth James. That day I think I read two small illustrated books, not understanding much. On our way home, I confessed to Dani that I could not decipher most of the words. Dani said I could have taken the books home and used a dictionary to find the meanings of the words I did not know. I had no idea what a dictionary was or how to use one. It was mind-boggling for me to discover that there was a way to find out the meaning of a word that I did not know. I had yet to see it done.

When we got to his house, Dani picked up an English-Amharic dictionary and started to show me how the words were organized (interestingly, we both were Eritreans speaking in Tigrinya, and yet we were using a dictionary that translated words from one foreign language to another). Dani asked me to spell a word I needed him to translate. I did so and he showed me how to look it up in Amharic. I was impressed, but Dani had to show me a few times before I got the hang of it.

For a couple of weeks, I was fascinated and amazed by the books I found in the library, so much that I completely forgot to study for my regular classes. I read so much during that week that I thought I knew everything there was to be known from reading books. Then I looked at the books Dani was reading and started to realize how much reading I would have to do in order to get to his level.

Following Dani's example, I started reading a book three times in order to fully understand a story. Initially, I would copy to a notebook the words I had trouble understanding. I would use the English-Amharic dictionary to translate each word. I would then translate the words from Amharic to Tigrinya in my head, and I would write in my notebook the meaning of each word in Tigrinya next to the English word. Finally, I would read the entire book again, but this time whenever I got to a new word, I would look at my notes to get a better understanding of the story.

Dani and his siblings had a few different versions and sizes of dictionaries on their bookshelf. One of the dictionaries that took my attention was a large blue Oxford English Dictionary. During one of our reading sessions, I asked Dani how he got the dictionary. Dani said, "My uncle Dr. Woldemichael sent it to me from Addis Ababa as a reward for my first-place prize."

"Really? You have a doctor uncle?" I was amazed to hear they had a doctor family member.

"Yes, he is my dad's older brother. He sends us a bunch of stuff every year when we tell him our school results. He is great," Dani added.

It is amazing the way our minds work. I paid very little attention to the reward, yet I was keen to hear about Dani's uncle and how he became a doctor. I probably had a more lavish lifestyle than Dani's family, with my dad and Aunt Abrehet showering me with clothing, a bicycle, soccer balls, games, and other toys from Saudi Arabia as rewards for my academic accomplishments. Yet here I was more interested to get information about becoming a doctor.

"Is that what you want to be when you grow up? I mean, a doctor like your uncle?" I asked Dani.

"I think so. What about you?"

"Well, I'm not really sure. I think I would love to be a doctor, but how do you become a one?" I asked Dani, hoping his uncle had shared with him the path.

"I don't know, Dawit. Let's think about it," said the ever-inquisitive Dani. "We will become teachers if we study biology or chemistry or physics. We might work in the bank if we study maths or accounting. You know my dad studied accounting?"

I'd never heard the term *accounting* before. I guessed there was more to life than the general sciences and maths.

"I don't think I want to become a teacher, considering the grief we give our teachers. I don't think I have the patience for that. Well, let's think about it. I love maths, but I hate biology and memorizing facts. I am actually using your notes to study for biology exams, but I don't need your notes for maths or physics," I told Dani.

"I think I will go for a doctor," Dani concluded, and I said, "Me, too." Only God knew how to get us there.

Dani and I talked a lot about becoming doctors. The only problem was that neither of us knew the path to pursue that career. For my part, deep inside, all I wanted was to finish university and get a degree in any field. The few times I had a chance to attend graduation ceremonies, I always came home motivated. I guess I could say that I actually saw myself graduating from Asmara University.

I introduced Dani to the Kifletzion family, whom I had met through Gebre Haile, one of my older brother Afewerki's friends. We started exchanging videotapes (mainly Indian movies) when the Kifletzion family would rent a movie from one of the shops in town for one week. Dani and I would rent different movies and then we would exchange the videotapes during the one-week period. Alem Kifletzion also had some Nintendo video games that had really impressed Dani, to the point he would ask me to take him to the Kifletzions' house more often than I would nag him for us to go to the British Council Library.

Dani also showed me how to play Monopoly, chess, and checkers, and in no time we started having matches. Thanks to the British version of the Monopoly board game and the books of Charles Dickens (*Oliver Twist, David Copperfield, A Christmas Carol...*), we made London our virtual vacation home. We basically were strolling through the streets of London without actually setting foot at Heathrow Airport. It is at this point that we started to live locally but think globally.

During our eighth-grade year, in 1988, Dani and I, along with a brilliant young female student named Aster Iyasu, were selected for a national academic competition representing Amanuel Elementary School. Both Dani and Aster had the sciences and the Amharic language covered, and they were relying on me for maths. We did very well during the morning and early afternoon sessions, and we made it to the finals.

As the competition progressed, it looked like whoever missed one question would take second place. It was our turn to answer the next question. The instructor asked a travel and distance word problem, where a boat was crossing a river and we had to determine the downstream speed of the boat given the speed of the current and the speed of the boat in still water. I was sure I had the answer. I did my calculation and yelled the answer with utmost confidence. The answer was wrong. I'd apparently used the wrong angle in my calculation. I blew it for the team.

The other team was given an opportunity to answer the question for an extra point, but they missed it as well. Our opponents answered their follow-up question correctly, and they won the trophy. We were in second place.

Aster and I did not really care much about the results. First, second or third place did not really make much of a difference for the two of us. We got a trophy and that was what mattered the most. The ever-competitive Dani, on the other hand, was devastated. Dani could never accept anything but first place. It probably took the rest of the day for him to cool down, but the next day we were back to our playing soccer outside Dani's house after playing chess or Monopoly or reading our favorite books.

In 1982, the Ethiopian dictator Mengistu Hailemariam declared his infamous Red Star Campaign in order to "repeat Ethiopia's victory over Somalia" in Eritrea. The Somali army had taken over Ogaden, historically disputed land between Ethiopia and Somalia, in 1977. This triggered the Ethio-Somali War, which lasted eight months, between July 1977 and March 1978. The war ended when the Ethiopian army pushed the Somali army out of Ogaden and advanced across the border, and the Somalis declared a truce that ended the war between the two nations.

In Eritrea, Mengistu Hailemariam wanted to destroy the "handful of bandits" and the "separatists" once and for all. Mengistu Hailemariam wanted his victory to go into the history books with documentation supporting his triumph. He wanted to make sure future Ethiopian generations remembered his accomplishments. He wanted to preserve the time-tested "Ethiopian unity" and ensure that he and only he would be able to resolve the question of Eritrea once and for all, an achievement none of his predecessors had been able to accomplish. He equipped his army with modern armaments supported by senior military advisers and strategists from Russia, Cuba, and Libya.

Mengistu Hailemariam hand-picked an experienced Ethiopian journalist as his propaganda chief for his Red

Star Campaign. Be'alu Girma was sent to document the an-nihilation of the "handful of bandits" and the closure of the "Eritrean question" once and for all.

The victories of the historic Red Star Campaign had to be documented. Be'alu Girma documented the entire cam-paign, from its inception, planning, and execution to its de-mise, in his book titled *Oromai*. Be'alu's book is in Amharic, yet he chose a fitting Tigrinya word for the title, which means "it is pointless." Using pseudonyms and fictitious characters, Be'alu documented and presented to his readers the Red Star Campaign in its entirety. From the Ethiopian army's perspec-tive, they were destroying the "bandits" and "liberating" the villages and towns the bandits were terrorizing.

The Ethiopian army believed they were pushing the bandits to their graves. Be'alu presented the details of the battlefield glo-ries of the victorious and heroic children of mother Ethiopia all the way to the mountains of Nakfa, in the Sahel region. Nakfa became the turning point of the war. The Ethiopian army was trapped in the rugged mountains there. Be'alu observed the slaughter of his comrades from a distance. He saw wave after wave of his comrades marching forward to the chain of moun-tains and hills of Nakfa, but the number of soldiers returning was minuscule. Be'alu used Hill 1702 as a metaphor for Nakfa, Sahel, or possibly Eritrea. The reporter decided to return to Asmara after seeing his countrymen crushed at Hill 1702.

Oromai was published in 1983, and it was banned twen-ty-four hours after its release. The government confiscated all copies it was able to collect from the various bookstores. Not long after, Be'alu Girma was executed by the Ethiopian secu-rity agents.

Be'alu Girma, the man who was sent to document history, did document the war in its ugliest form and realized the war was indeed pointless—*Oromai*. Yet it took a decade of warfare and the bloodshed of hundreds of thousands of human beings for Ethiopian politicians and the rest of the world to realize the futility of Ethiopia's aggression.

In 1983, a few months after Ethiopia's much-heralded sixth offensive (a continuation of the Red Star Campaign) was soundly defeated by the Eritrean freedom fighters in the mountains of Sahel, Haggai Erlich, an Israeli historian and expert on the Tigrean warlord Alula, made this prediction: "The Eritrean organizations were not destroyed, but their chances of defeating the Ethiopian armed forces and recapturing Eritrea became remote. What had seemed just a year earlier a feasible military option for fulfilling Eritrean nationalism was rendered impossible and seems likely to remain so for the foreseeable future... Eritrean victory may realistically be excluded as a future possibility. The chances of those identified with Eritrean nationalism achieving it by military victory over the Ethiopian armed forces seem very remote."[25]

To the contrary, the Eritrean freedom fighters' strategic withdrawal was a success. The armed struggle did not get crushed. It survived and crushed Africa's largest army, which was armed to the teeth and supported by senior military advisers and strategists from Russia, Cuba, Libya, and later from the United States.

Between 1978 and 1986, the Ethiopian army launched eight unsuccessful major offensives against the Eritrean

25 Erlich, Haggai. *The Struggle Over Eritrea, 1962–1978: War and Revolution in the Horn of Africa*. Stanford, Calif.: Hoover Institution Press, 1983.

freedom fighters. By 1986, the Ethiopian government had increased the intensity of the conscription of Eritrean youth. But the "bandits" were actually Eritrean freedom fighters, who were at least our relatives if not our fathers, uncles, aunts, brothers, or sisters.

THE TURNING POINT
FOR ASMARA

"I dream of giving birth to a child who will ask,
'Mother, what was war?'" —Eve Merriam

Between the fall of 1985 and the summer of 1989, Dani and I read the books at the British Council Library from wall to wall. Some of the authors we read during those years included Agatha Christie, Charles Dickens, Sir Arthur Conan Doyle, Henry Rider Haggard, Robert Louis Stevenson, Jonathan Swift, Mark Twain, Jules Verne, and of course, Ian Fleming's James Bond series. Sometimes we visited the American Library for reference books, for which the library was widely known among its customers.

Not all our adventures took place at the library. During those years we also began to enjoy Western music by Michael Jackson, Billy Ocean, Madonna, Stevie Wonder, Dolly Parton, Don Williams, Lionel Richie, Kenny Rogers, Kool & the Gang, Boney M, the legendary Bob Marley, and, of course, the "Candy Licker" Marvin Sease, among others. We borrowed audiotapes from friends and copied them. We would transcribe the lyrics to the best of our ability by listening to the tapes and then singing along. We used to miss some words and phrases here and there, but for the major part, we did get the lyrics right. My favorite and most memorable song was Kool & the Gang's "Fresh":

> *Conversation is going round*
>> *People talking 'bout the girl who's come to town*
> *Lovely lady pretty as can be*
>> *No one knows her name she's just a mystery*
> *I have seen her maybe once or twice*
>> *The one thing I can say though she's very nice*
> *She's a lady—one I really want to know*
>> *Somehow I've got to let my feelings show*

With a gesture of kindness and encouragement, Aboy Mebrahtu Negusse had opened wide the door of knowledge for me. I dearly respected and envied him. I adopted him as a father and he adopted me as a son. The greatest English novelist of the Victorian period, Charles Dickens, wrote in *Great Expectations*, "In the little world in which children have their existence whosoever brings them up, there is nothing so finely perceived and so finely felt, as injustice."

Well, conversely, I also do not think there is anything so finely perceived and so finely felt by children as a gesture of goodwill.

I passed both fifth and sixth grades, for which I was enrolled in that single year, without any difficulty and did well in my sixth-grade matriculation exam. Unfortunately, when I went to register for seventh grade at Amanuel Elementary, the director refused to register me. I was turned down by the school I had attended since kindergarten.

"What am I going to tell your classmates if I allow you to skip sixth grade?" was the director's answer to my request.

I tried to explain that I had not skipped, but that I had attended and passed sixth grade with high marks. He refused to budge, telling me that I would need to go to night school and that there would be no school willing to take me for a day shift. I could not understand why this man, whom I had admired for many years for his dedication to his students, would think I had become a bad example by attending two grades in one year. I really would not have had a problem repeating sixth grade at Amanuel had I done poorly on the national general examination. My problem was that I had scored in the top 2 or 3 percent on the exam. With that score, I thought any school would accept me. I could not have been more wrong!

I went home and I told Mom what had happened. She sent me to talk to Aunt Abrehet, who had recently come from Saudi Arabia, in the hope that she might know someone who could help me. Aunt Abrehet talked to Memhr Melake, who was able to get me registered into seventh grade at Selam (Peace) Elementary and Junior Secondary School, in the regular day shift. The disadvantage was that the school was far from where I lived, and I had to walk forty to forty-five minutes every day to get there. In addition, class started at seven fifteen a.m., much earlier than most schools in the city. That meant that I had to get up at five thirty in order to eat breakfast and leave home by six fifteen.

During my seventh-grade year, 1986–87, I spent most of the weekends with my cousins Zemichael and Tesfalem Negash, Tedros Simon, Yonas Tsegay, and Mengisteab Yohanes playing cards and listening to *Voice of the Broad Masses of Eritrea* (a.k.a. *Voice of the Masses*), a clandestine radio program operated by the EPLF Information Division, Deutsche Welle (Germany's international broadcasting service), and the Voice of America. We were also dubbing audiotapes containing revolutionary songs that were outlawed by the Ethiopian government. *Voice of the Masses* did a great job in strengthening the youth's Eritrean identity and demystifying the Ethiopian government's effort to force-feed us the "three-thousand-year history of Ethiopia" that included Eritrea and the Red Sea.

Voice of the Masses was like a breath of fresh air compared to the suffocation we felt by the day in, day out Ethiopian propaganda machine—Ethiopian television, radio programs in Amharic and other Eritrean languages, Ethiopian patriotic songs produced by famous Ethiopian musicians, pamphlets, and other political materials. Each Ethiopian singer was required to have one or more patriotic songs on every album released. There were weekly and monthly organizational meetings at the district and zonal levels as platforms for political awareness by the Ethiopian cadres. Middle school through high school students were required to take and pass one class/subject of political education every year. All school-age students were required to line up in front of their schools at the beginning and end of the school day to recite the Ethiopian national anthem and the Amharic version of "The Internationale," the official anthem of the Comintern (Communist International) that ends with "the Internationale will be the human race."

By 1988, some of the best news to the people of Eritrea was broadcast all over the world: much of the Ethiopian army in Eritrea—the Nadew (Amharic for "demolish it") Command unit—had been totally defeated during the largest-ever EPLF offensive, resulting in the liberation of the northern and western parts of Eritrea. During this battle, the Eritrean People's Liberation Front captured 130-millimeter Russian artilleries and BM-21s, Russian-made multiple rocket launchers nicknamed "Stalin's organ" after Soviet leader Joseph Stalin. The BM-21 fires forty rockets through its four tiers of ten tubes. The EPLF later was able to modify the BM-21 by breaking up the four tiers of ten tubes to make ten tiers of four tubes. This modification of the armament was very cost-effective for the guerrilla fighters, allowing them to load and fire only four instead of forty rockets at a time. It was also a testament to the ingenuity of the Eritrean freedom fighters that had been discounted and trivialized by the superpowers and the international community as a "handful of rebels." That handful of rebels managed to capture three senior Russian military advisers, who were later handed over to the Red Cross.

Some twenty thousand Ethiopian troops were killed, and tens of thousands of captured were handed over to the Red Cross. The British journalist and African historian Basil Davidson described the Eritreans' victory on this front as "the most significant conventional battle in the third world since

2

the Vietnamese liberation forces defeated the French at Dien Bien Phu."[26]

The Ethiopian army responded to its military defeat by raiding houses and performing house-to-house searches in Asmara. One Sunday morning, Mom woke us up abruptly at five a.m. We were shocked and confused. We got dressed quickly and sat together nervously, waiting for Mom to tell us what was going on. Grandpa Tecle told us that Ethiopian soldiers had surrounded the entire city. Grandpa, who did not live with us but who had come to Asmara the day before to shop, had gotten up at four thirty that morning to attend the early church service. His plan was to be back from church by nine a.m. and to return to his village in the afternoon. Fortunately for us, he had gotten only a block away when the Ethiopian soldiers sent him back, telling him not to leave the house for the rest of the day.

Before Grandpa even finished speaking, Mom turned to me. I tried to avoid her eyes, but it was impossible. I knew what she suspected. She was not sure, but as any mother of an Eritrean teen would, she suspected I might be in possession of literature or audiotapes with information about the Eritrean armed struggle—which were outlawed by the Ethiopian government. I got up and went to the drawer next to my bed. I pulled out a handful of Eritrean patriotic audiotapes. The shock on her face was obvious. Yet she calmly asked me if there was anything else. I said yes, there was another videotape.

Now she went ballistic. She asked what videotape I was talking about. Grandpa stepped in and tried to calm her

26   Cliffe, Lionel, and Basil Davidson, eds., *The Long Struggle of Eritrea for Independence and Constructive Peace.* Trenton, NJ: Red Sea Press, 1988.

down, saying it was not the time for a tantrum. It was time to get rid of, or hide, whatever was there. I went to the room we had started using as a living room after one of the tenants left and brought back two tapes of my cousin's wedding in Saudi Arabia. I also retrieved a videotape of the Eritrean People's Liberation Front Unity Congress of 1987. The lyrics of the songs in the videotape were forecasting the end of Ethiopian colonization while glorifying the heroism of the Eritrean freedom fighters. If the Ethiopian soldiers were to find the tapes in our possession, the entire family would have landed in a maximum-security prison—or been shot. Mom kept praying while threatening me at the same time.

By now, my oldest brother, Afewerki, had made it to the United States. My sisters, Lemlem, Simret, Akberet, and baby Tigisti, were sitting next to my grandpa, grabbing his clothing with a great deal of fear. We all watched my mom as she walked frantically back and forth across the room, talking aimlessly. She came near me and started uttering words—we could not tell whether Mom was praying or threatening me, God, or his disciples. Mom was mixing everything up. Thanks to Grandpa's unrelenting patience, I was able to concentrate on my search for every outlawed piece of material. I was able to find all the audio and videotapes that contained Eritrean revolutionary songs, recorded mostly from the *Voice of the Masses* radio show.

I placed them all in three separate plastic bags. Following Grandpa's instructions, I went outside to the garden, pushed aside dry leaves and grass, and dug a hole. I buried the plastic bags, put two small bricks on top of them, and then put back the soil and leaves. I made sure the ground was level and took some of the leftover dirt to a different spot in the yard. Then I went back to the house and we sat down. Mom had cooled down a bit by this time and was praying for the day to end in peace.

Sometime around nine a.m., the soldiers came to check our compound, starting with the first house. When it was our turn, they were thorough in their search of all the rooms we were occupying, starting under our beds and moving on to the closets and the drawers.

One of the soldiers went to the utensils cabinet and started picking up the teacups and the smaller coffee cups. He went through each cup by picking up and flipping it upside down, two cups together at times. The other two started going through our clothing in the two-door closet. They also kept randomly looking under our bed frames. They then picked up each bed and turned it upside down.

They left without finding anything. We sat in silence, shaken, staring at each other. We were weak with relief. My mother broke down, clutching all her children to her breast, tearfully thanking God for sparing our family.

Years later, when I went home after years in exile, one of the first things I did was dig up those buried tapes. To my disappointment, I found everything decayed. My biggest disappointment was the loss of my cousin's wedding tapes—buried so hastily and without any sort of covering or container to protect them. The wedding ceremony had been one of the most culturally rich festivities I had seen at the time. In my view, that tape was a testimony to the Eritrean expatriates' masterful adaptation of their culture. In Eritrea, for example, people clap their hands during parties and celebrations, while

Eritreans in Saudi Arabia designed two wooden clapping tools so the sound of the claps matched the level of the machine drum. Everyone in the wedding was dressed in the traditional way. I had never seen that many people in one place dressed in the Eritrean cultural attire. It was beautiful.

The plight of Eritreans during that next year did not end with the now routine house-to-house searches. The Ethiopian government also arrested and persecuted many civilian residents of Asmara. In addition, the Ethiopians increased their draft campaign, aggressively conscripting students from high schools and marketplaces for military service—taking people right off the street. These recruits were meant to replace the soldiers the Ethiopian army had lost in battles the previous year.

On the afternoon of May 16, 1989, our teacher suddenly told us that a state of emergency had been declared across the country. We were let out of school early.

When the teacher let us out around three that afternoon, he did not give us any details about what had happened, and we did not ask. But as we rushed out of the school compound, we saw soldiers on top of a military vehicle in full battle armor, looking left and right. We stopped in our tracks and pressed our backs against the wall of the compound. What we saw was frightening—a soldier tied to the back of the armored vehicle by a rope around his neck, looking as if he were sleeping in an awkward position. He was upside down, being dragged behind the truck. That vehicle was followed by four other trucks. The fourth truck was dragging another soldier. The soldiers getting dragged on the streets were top commanders of the army, who had staged a coup d'état against the Ethiopian dictator Mengistu Hailemariam. The coup had been crushed in the wee hours of that morning.

When the vehicles had gone out of sight, the road they had passed over was covered in blood.

I followed my first instinct and went over to Amanuel Public Elementary School to pick up my sisters Simret and Akberet. To my surprise, the school compound was deserted.

When I got home, I found my mom and the neighbors standing outside. Before I could finish greeting them, my mom asked in an enraged tone where I had been. I told her that I had gone looking for Simret and Akberet. Furious, she started shouting at me in a tone I had never heard before. I asked why she was talking to me like that. She said, "What do I have to gain by losing all of you?" When we got inside and she cooled down, she told me from that time on, in any emergency, my job was to get myself to safety and let God worry about my siblings.

She gathered all of us together in the bedroom, and we pretty much sat in silence listening to the radio for the rest of the evening. However, there was no news about the events of the day.

The situation in Asmara continued to worsen, and by the end of June 1989, the Ethiopian government declared another conscription campaign. At this point, my parents decided that the best thing would be for us to leave the country.

The first thought was to go to the Sudan, but that option was dropped immediately because of the high concentration of the Ethiopian army near the Eritrea–Sudan border, which would make the trip dangerous. The other option was to go to Addis Ababa, the capital city of Ethiopia, where Aya Mohammed Kelifa Adem Hasebu of Adi-Hayo was living with his family, and then leave for Kenya. After much deliberation, we decided the Addis Ababa route would be the safest option, although it entailed entering the belly of the beast.

Initially, Lemlem was sent to Addis Ababa to stay with Aya Mohammed's family, and I was to follow soon after.

A few weeks later, Zemichael Negash, Tedros Simon, Mengisteab Yohanes, and I were celebrating the feast of Pagume, the celebration of the last five days of the liturgical year. Following tradition, most people go to the compound of Mai Timqet (the water of Epiphany) after church. But we got together at our house in the morning and went there around noon. Once we got there, we joined the crowd, saw some people we knew, and kept striding toward the center of the compound, where people were filling tins with blessed water. One of us—I do not now remember who—grabbed a can of water and splashed the others. We all reacted, laughing and cursing, and looked for containers so that we could splash in turn. We started running and splashing. We were unprepared for what happened next. One of the Ethiopian revolutionary guards at the compound grabbed Tedros by the shirt. We all gathered around the guard, who was yelling and shouting at Tedros. Tedros protested that he was just playing with us. But before we knew it, we were surrounded by four guards. They told us to follow them toward the pole where the Ethiopian flag was flying. We started to panic, not knowing what we had done wrong or why the guards were pushing and shoving us.

At the pole, the guard told us to kneel down beneath the flag. The guard holding Tedros pushed him against the pole and told him he would make him bleed. Tedros, true to his nature, instead of quietly kneeling beside us, looked back at the guard and muttered a few words under his breath. The guard grabbed Tedros by his neck and punched him in the face. We all moved to rescue Tedros but had to fall back when the rest of the guards started beating us with their rubber sticks. We tried to run, but before we knew it we were surrounded by even more national guards, giving us no choice but to go back and kneel down at the pole as we had been instructed. Tedros, by this time, was spitting blood. One of his teeth had been knocked loose. A soldier from the regular army approached and spoke to one of the guards. This new soldier told us to get to our feet, bow to the flag, and ask for forgiveness from the revolutionary guard. We stared at each other with amazement but realized there was no other way out. We bowed, as instructed, and asked for forgiveness in Amharic. Finally we were allowed to leave.

As far as we were concerned, we had done nothing wrong on that beautiful, sunny day of Pagume, the end-of-year celebration. All we had been doing was playing and running around. But apparently, Eritrean youngsters enjoying themselves in our city had come to be considered criminals by the Ethiopian government. As the memory of a teenager is short-lived, we tended to forget most of the unwritten rules governing our country. It did not take long, though, to run into circumstances that would remind us of the rules. For most of us, all we had to endure was humiliation and a few sticks on our backs. Tedros Simon had to pay with the loss of one of his teeth.

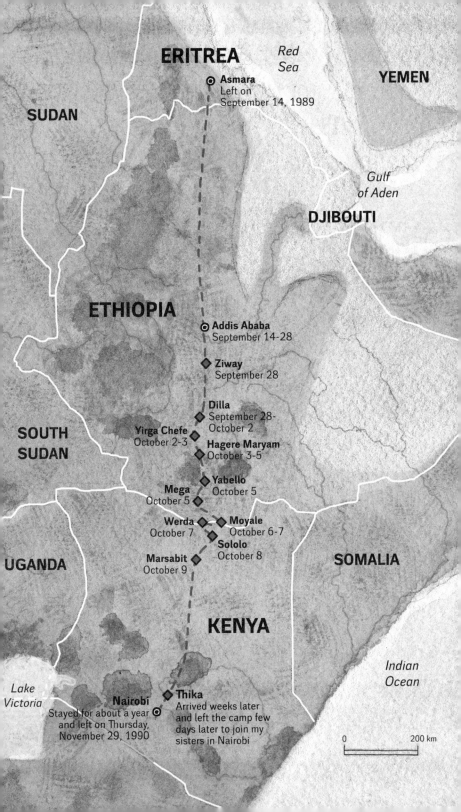

ERITREA

Red Sea

YEMEN

SUDAN

◎ **Asmara**
Left on
September 14, 1989

Gulf of Aden

DJIBOUTI

ETHIOPIA

◎ **Addis Ababa**
September 14-28

◆ **Ziway**
September 28

SOUTH SUDAN

◆ **Dilla**
September 28-
October 2

Yirga Chefe
October 2-3

◆ **Hagere Maryam**
October 3-5

◆ **Yabello**
October 5

Mega
October 5

◆ **Werda**
October 7

◆ **Moyale**
October 6-7

◆ **Sololo**
October 8

Marsabit
October 9

UGANDA

SOMALIA

KENYA

Indian Ocean

Lake Victoria

◆ **Thika**
Arrived weeks later
and left the camp few
days later to join my
sisters in Nairobi

Nairobi
Stayed for about a year
and left on Thursday,
November 29, 1990

0   200 km

HUMAN SMUGGLING

"No matter what sort of difficulties, how painful experience is, if we lose our hope, that's our real disaster." —Dalai Lama XIV

Before leaving home I did something I had never done before: I bought a small journal to carry with me to my unknown destination. The journal, known as an *awde awarh* (pocket calendar, in the ancient Geez language), included both the Gregorian and Geez calendars. The new year of the Geez calendar (also known as the Coptic, or Julian, calendar) starts on September 11 (or 12 during the Julian calendar's leap year). The calendar has twelve months of thirty days each, followed by an extra five days (six days in a leap year). In addition to the list of holidays, the *awde awarh* contained motivational quotations at the bottom of each page. Before beginning that trip, I do not remember carrying *awde awarh* for either religious or scheduling reasons. I was neither a devotee of the rigorous fasting and the many holidays observed by the Eastern Orthodox Church nor an organized person who had yet felt the need for a calendar. For this trip, however, I did carry an *awde awarh,* and I protected it almost to the degree that I protected my life. I read its motivational quotations whenever I needed something to hold on to for support. From now on, I will refer to it as my notebook.

At almost fifteen years old, I had no clue what the future held for me. My past had been as healthy, fun filled, and productive as a young boy growing up in a small city could ask for. That past had now come to an abrupt end due to circumstances beyond my control. I had to leave my family, my country, my city, and my past life to start a journey to an unknown destination. The future seemed dim and full of uncertainties.

This was September 14, 1989 (September 4, 1982, according to the Geez calendar). That Thursday at four a.m. Lemlem's best friend and my brother's future wife, Eden Tewelde Ogbagebriel, and I were at Asmara Airport waiting for a six a.m. flight.

Eden, who lived in the third house north of us in Asmara, is light skinned with long hair, and average height—about the same height as Lemlem. She and Lemlem became inseparable childhood friends in no time. Eden by nature is quiet and a person of few words. Most of the time, Eden would bring Tigrinya or Amharic fiction books to our house to share with Lemlem. I was sure Lemlem was sharing tales and stories with Eden, considering no one could hear them when they were alone in one corner of the stairs in front of our house.

Even though the Ethiopian government had renamed the airport the Yohanes IV International Airport, in honor of the Ethiopian emperor, Eritreans continued to refer to it as Asmara Airport. It is located in the southwestern outskirts of Asmara. At the time, to most Eritreans, including myself, the airport seemed like one of the fanciest places on earth. As I vaguely remember, the entrance had two sliding doors and huge, impressive mirrors all over the building. We used to watch for incoming guests from the airport cafeteria on the first floor. This time, though, I was on the other side of the view: inside the customs area.

I felt estranged in my own land. I was carrying a forged identification card. It showed my real name and picture but the wrong address, thanks to Uncle Yohanes, who had secured it for me. The card listed a village outside the city as the place where I had been born and raised. I wondered at the time if I would be doomed to the same fate as my father: a life in exile.

We got our suitcase weighed and picked up our boarding passes from the ticket counter. Once we arrived at the passengers' waiting room, Eden and I sat next to each other to wait for our flight's departure. Suddenly, I turned around and was shocked and surprised to see Dani's father, Aboy Mebrahtu Negusse, my mentor and the man who had welcomed me into his house and his family for many years. I reacted as if I had seen a ghost. Seconds later, Aboy Mebrahtu looked up and saw me staring at him. He came to where we were sitting and greeted us. After we exchanged greetings, Aboy Mebrahtu asked me the question I was praying he would not ask, but he surely must ask, considering we both were in an airport. Aboy Mebrahtu asked me where I was going, and I told him I was going to visit Addis Ababa for a couple of weeks. I couldn't look at his face. I could not tell Aboy Mebrahtu that I was leaving the country, because he knew it was impossible for anyone of Eritrean origin to leave the country legally. If I were to tell Aboy Mebrahtu I was planning to go to Kenya, he would wonder how I obtained an exit visa to leave Ethiopia.

After I uttered the few words to Aboy Mebrahtu, knowing that I was lying, my eyes started wandering all over the place. If I were Pinocchio, I am sure my nose would have grown to a record length. I lied to the man who had not only welcomed me to his home but also adopted me as his firstborn son. But I convinced myself he was better off not knowing. Without realizing it, I seemed to have started living the complex immigrant life of sharing information on a need-to-know basis.

And here we were both leaving our beloved city. Aboy Mebrahtu was sure of his destination and return date. He was going to Addis Ababa for two weeks. I, on the other hand, was sure of neither my destination nor my return date, or if I would ever return.

When we heard the announcement to start boarding the plane, we joined the line that was forming. When our turn came, they let Aboy Mebrahtu in, but the airline personnel told Eden and me that we had to wait until our names were called. Aboy Mebrahtu wished us well and said he would see me when I got back to Asmara. Little did he know that years were going to pass before we would see each other and speak face-to-face again! Eden and I went back to our seats without saying anything.

We were called to board three more times. Each time our stomachs churned with apprehension. Eden and I were near fainting by the time we were told to wait for the next flight— scheduled for six p.m.—because the plane was full.

While we waited, I became restless. I told myself that I could not believe what I had done. I started thinking about the many things Aboy Mebrahtu had done for me, and how much he trusted me since the day we first met. He welcomed me into his house. He helped me discover books and an amazing library. He treated me like a son. But I needed to keep my travel plans secret.

Aboy Mebrahtu's upbringing and his personal drive for academic success are testimony to his generation's determination and drive for excellence. Born to his father, Negusse Hagos, and his mother, Letekidan Habtemichael, Aboy Mebrahtu's life spans the various colonial eras of modern-day Eritrea: the Italians, the British military administration, the nominal federal union with Ethiopia, and the successive Ethiopian colonial administrations.

Aboy Mebrahtu Negusse was born during the Italian colonization of Eritrea on May 22, 1933, in Asmara, Eritrea. At the end of WWII, the Italians were defeated by the Allied forces, and Eritrea was handed over to the British military administration (BMA) until the fate of the inhabitants was decided by the League of Nations, which later became the United Nations. The BMA became the custodian of Eritrea while retaining Italian civil services.

A teenage Mebrahtu completed his middle school education with distinction. He then took an examination for entry to higher education sponsored by the BMA. Aboy Mebrahtu and two other Eritrean students from Comboni Middle School and three other students from the famous Biete Georgis (St. George) Middle School passed the examination and were offered partial scholarships to attend a boarding school in Khartoum, Sudan. The scholarship provided by BMA covered 50 percent of the total expenses for tuition, room, and board.

The parents of each student were expected to come up with the remaining 50 percent of the expense. Unfortunately for Aboy Mebrahtu, his parents were not able to afford the portion of the fee expected from them. The meager salary Aboy Mebrahtu's dad was earning could barely sustain a family of seven school-aged children in a city supposedly built as a replica of Rome, both in structural design and its residents' lifestyle.

Comboni's school administration noticed Aboy Mebrahtu's academic excellence and his examination results and decided to help him achieve his goal of attending the boarding school in Khartoum. The school administration designed a program for Aboy Mebrahtu to come back to Comboni and teach for a year in exchange for the school to cover his portion of the fee. Aboy Mebrahtu signed a promissory note to repay the school by teaching at his alma mater after completing his four years of education in Khartoum.

After four years of study, he returned to Asmara. To fulfill his obligation, Aboy Mebrahtu started teaching at his alma mater, Comboni Elementary School. His family was still not in a position to help him afford proper clothing and shoes. Shoes were a luxury, considering the family's meager and stagnant income.

After teaching at Comboni for a year and half, at the end of 1954, Aboy Mebrahtu secured a job at the State Bank of Ethiopia in Asmara for two hundred Ethiopian birr per month, twice the salary his dad was earning as a clerk at the court. Aboy Mebrahtu's life completely changed for the better. Not only could he afford shoes, he also had to wear suits and ties in order to adhere to the formal dress code required for bank officials.

Two years into his life as an accountant at the State Bank of Ethiopia, he read an advertisement by the American consulate inviting any high school graduates to take the university entrance examination. Those who did well in the exam were guaranteed entry to the American University in Beirut, Lebanon.

Initially, Aboy Mebrahtu did not pay that much attention to the advertisement. He was very comfortable with the lifestyle he had at the time and did not remotely consider further education.

On the day the exam was given, Aboy Mebrahtu went to his office just like any other day. Once in the office, though, he did not find anything of urgency. While looking for something to read, he saw the advertisement on his desk and noticed that the exam was given at Model Elementary School across the street. Since it was a slow day in the office, he went to Model Elementary School and took the exam.

When Aboy Mebrahtu went to check his results at the US consulate, he was shocked to find out that he had scored the highest marks, followed by Emanuel Amde Michael, who later became administrator general of Eritrea and minister of justice under the military junta that overthrew Emperor Haile Selassie of Ethiopia. Then, reality dawned on Aboy Mebrahtu. He was not sure he could actually quit his current job and leave his family destitute in order for him to continue his education. If Aboy Mebrahtu left his job at the bank, the family would be back to having only his father's limited income of one hundred birr per month. A number of his siblings were also in school at the time.

Mr. Wigner, a Norwegian who was managing the State Bank of Ethiopia, went to Aboy Mebrahtu's office to congratulate him on his results. Aboy Mebrahtu thanked his boss and told him he was not planning to go because of his family situation. Mr. Wigner naturally asked if there was anything he could do to help. Aboy Mebrahtu told his boss the best and only help he could accept would be if Mr. Wigner allowed Aboy Mebrahtu's younger brother Habtom to work at the bank. Mr. Wigner asked Aboy Mebrahtu if his brother had graduated from high school. The answer was no. Mr. Wigner then asked if his brother knew how to type. Again, the response was no. Mr. Wigner thought about the predicament his best employee was putting him in and finally told Aboy Mebrahtu to bring his brother to the bank and start training him to type. While making the necessary preparations for his trip to Beirut, Lebanon, Aboy Mebrahtu started training his brother, who was in eleventh grade at the time. Habtom excelled in mastering the typing machine and secured a job at the State Bank of Eritrea, taking over Aboy Mebrahtu's responsibilities helping his family.

Between 1956 and 1960, Aboy Mebrahtu studied at the American University in Beirut with full scholarship and a stipend in the amount of one hundred US dollars to cover room and board. By saving from the one-hundred-dollar stipend, Aboy Mebrahtu and his colleagues spent their first summer vacation traveling to Damascus, Istanbul, Ankara, and southern parts of Turkey. During the summer after their second year, the team traveled to Europe via boat. At the end of their third year, the three Eritrean students went back home for vacation. The US consulate paid for their airfares.

Once back in Asmara with a bachelor's degree in public administration, Aboy Mebrahtu and the other two students were sent to Addis Ababa, Ethiopia, to give their respect to the king. They all were given instructions on how to handle themselves in the presence of the king.

During their meeting with the king, each of the three honorees was asked where he wanted to work, and Aboy Mebrahtu responded by saying he wanted to go back to Asmara and help his family. The king, however, noting Aboy Mebrahtu's lack of fluency in Amharic, Ethiopia's official language, ridiculed Aboy Mebrahtu by saying, "You are able to speak many foreign languages with fluency and have trouble speaking in the language of your motherland."

The king then ordered Aboy Mebrahtu to work in Addis Ababa for one year in order to learn the Amharic language and to return to Asmara only after he'd mastered it. Aboy Mebrahtu worked at the State Bank of Ethiopia in Addis Ababa for ten months, but his stay was shortened due to the unrest in Ethiopia as a result of Mengstu Neway's unsuccessful attempt to overthrow the emperor that took place in December 1960. At the same time, Aboy Mebrahtu also started speaking the Amharic language with some level of fluency.

From 1961 through 1966, Aboy Mebrahtu again worked at the State Bank of Ethiopia in Asmara. In 1966, he was approached by Haregot Abay, the mayor of Asmara from 1963 to 1974, to work at the Asmara municipality as head of finance, replacing an Italian official who'd held the position since the colonial era. After working for about four years as head of finance, Aboy Mebrahtu became the director general of finance under Mayor Haregot Abay. At this time, Emperor Haile Selassie awarded Aboy Mebrahtu a military title of qenyazmach, commander of the right wing of the Ethiopian armed forces.

In 1974, Emperor Haile Selassie was overthrown by a military junta that called itself the Derg ("committee" in Amharic). The Derg detained and executed Haregot Abay in 1974.

Demisie Banjaw, of Ethiopian origin and Asmara's deputy mayor, became the acting mayor. One of the directives of the newly appointed acting mayor was the destruction of the eucalyptus forest in the area of Biete Georgis. Demisie Banjaw's rationale was that the "bandits," as the Ethiopians referred to the Eritrean freedom fighters, were using the forest as a hiding and planning place for their operations in Asmara. To that end, he sent a team to start cutting eucalyptus trees and selling them in the wood market. There was a problem with Demisie Banjaw's directives and implementation plan—he was not providing any type of receipts to the Department of Finance. Consistent with his responsibilities and duties as director general of finance, Aboy Mebrahtu Negusse submitted a letter to his new boss asking him for receipts of the eucalyptus trees that were getting sold by the municipality. The acting mayor retaliated against Aboy Mebrahtu by having him arrested. Aboy Mebrahtu was detained for about a month and released after the court cleared him of any wrongdoing. True to his nature, Aboy Mebrahtu persistently followed up on his inquiry for the receipts of the trees that were sold by the municipality. He submitted a formal request for inquiry on the disbursement of the proceeds collected from the sales of the eucalyptus. Once the mayor was notified of the formal investigation that was underway, his friends in the Ethiopian Air Force whisked the mayor off to Addis Ababa.

While working as director general of finance in Asmara, in 1976, Aboy Mebrahtu started teaching accounting on a part-time basis at the Haile Selassie I University, on the evening shift. In 1978, Aboy Mebrahtu also started teaching part-time at Asmara University. Finally, in 1980, Aboy Mebrahtu left the Department of Finance at the Municipality and joined Asmara University as a full-time lecturer and head of administration. By this time, Aboy Mebrahtu fluently spoke Tigrinya (his native language), Amharic, Italian, and English.

In 1982, Aboy Mebrahtu went to Università degli Studi di Torino (the University of Turin), in the city of Torino, in northwestern Italy, for his master's. In 1984, he returned to Asmara with a master's degree in business administration and became the dean of social science at Asmara University.

Aboy Mebrahtu was the dean when I approached him to help me get library cards. Considering his background and the many hurdles he had to jump over to achieve academic excellence, it's no wonder Aboy Mebrahtu welcomed me to his home with open arms. He must have seen in me a reflection of himself when he was studying at Comboni. Aboy Mebrahtu Negusse is a man I grew to admire both as an intellectual and as a family man, who took a great deal of pride in taking care of his kids.

Incidentally, I was attending Comboni Elementary and Middle School, Aboy Mebrahtu's elementary school, when we met. During Aboy Mebrahtu's days, Comboni was privately run by the Comboni missionaries. By the time I was there for sixth grade, the school had been nationalized by the Ethiopian military government.

Eden and I stayed at Asmara Airport for the rest of the day, finally getting out on the six p.m. flight to Addis Ababa. We also met one of my cousins, Samson Tesfamichael, who was taking the six p.m. flight to Addis Ababa. Samson asked the same question Aboy Mebrahtu Negusse had asked earlier that day: Where was I going? I gave him the same answer: I was going to visit Addis Ababa for a couple of weeks. On a need-to-know basis.

We arrived in Addis Ababa about an hour later, only to find that Mohammed Kelifa was not there to meet us. He had been expecting us on the morning flight, and we guessed that he had finally left the airport when we did not arrive on the next several incoming flights. Luckily, cousin Samson, who knew his way around the city, was able to take us to Mohammed Kelifa's house by taxi.

The two weeks we spent in Addis Ababa were eye-opening for me. The Ethiopian capital was much larger than Asmara. There was continuous rain, which was also unusual for someone coming from Asmara. I found one of my cousins, Biniam Abraham, who had been living in the city for a couple of years to escape getting drafted to the army, and I spent most of my time with him. Biniam was one of the family members and friends whom I felt comfortable letting in on the secret of why we were in Addis Ababa. I also needed his help—on a need-to-know basis.

To my shock and dismay, after I told Biniam of our plans to go to Kenya through Ethiopia, he turned around and told his aunt. In those days it was common for people to ask travelers to deliver money to relatives in far-flung cities. So when Biniam took me to his aunt's house, she asked me to take fifty US dollars to her son, who had gone to Kenya six months earlier. To his credit, Biniam had not been foolish enough to tell her the whole story, so the poor lady did not know the details of our trip. I tried to make excuses, telling her it would be nearly impossible for me to find her son in a place as vast as Nairobi. But she insisted on taking the chance, saying only, "Don't worry, you will find him."

After we left the house, I turned on Biniam and started yelling at him. "Are you crazy, Biniam?" I asked. "You know we will be crossing the border illegally!"

I tried to hand over the money to Biniam, telling him to return it to his aunt. He refused, saying he did not want to jeopardize his relationship with the old lady. I was furious. After that incident, I decided not to share our plan of going to Nairobi with anyone.

I decided to put the money in the small pocket in the top part of my underwear and let it share my fate. If I made it to Nairobi in one piece, I was sure the fifty-dollar bill was going to make it to its intended destination as well. For some odd reason, though, Biniam's aunt was convinced the money would reach her son.

Two weeks after our arrival in Addis Ababa, on Thursday, September 28, at six a.m., we started the long journey to Nairobi, Kenya. The locals referred to this journey as camel flight, implying an arduous trek, like a camel going through the desert. Mohammed Kelifa took me and Eden, along with

Lemlem—who had been waiting for us in Addis Ababa—to one of the bus stations, and there we met a man whose business was getting people across the border from Ethiopia to Kenya. The name of the human smuggler was Tesfaye.

Tesfaye led us to one of the buses parked at the station, an open area with a lot of people continuously moving back and forth. We boarded the bus that was heading toward Dilla, a city in the southern part of Ethiopia. The bus was already full of passengers, and the driver was waving for us to hurry. Tesfaye led us to our seats and sat at the front near the driver.

The landscape and the scenery in southern Ethiopia were breathtaking. I tried looking as far away as my eyes would allow, and all I could see was an endless green, dense forest. After a while, we reached flat terrain. I had never before seen a landscape this beautiful. Many Ethiopians and tourists love to travel along this road to swim in Ethiopia's rift valley lakes. For us, though, this was not a vacation trip. It was a lifesaving mission.

On the radio, an Amharic song by an Ethiopian singer named Yeshimebet Dubale was playing:

Having the abundance of fruit in the east and dairy in the
south, coffee in the west, and crops in the north,
    The vast national wealth of all varieties,
Why, my countryman, suffer in exile?
    Pride of one's self better come from within
Rather than from the comfort and joy of living in someone
else's terrain.
    Instead of living away from home longing for country's kin,

> *Instead of living in someone else's land reviled and despised*
> *Instead of living as alien in a foreign land,*
> *Hungry or full, you are better off in your ancestral land.*

Other lyrics were full of pitiful stories about life in exile. It felt like the driver knew exactly where we were headed and was preparing us for our future life. That music hit me at my core.

We stopped for lunch at a coffee shop in a small town called Ziway. When we sat down to eat, something very strange happened. There were about twenty of us sitting in a circle to eat. But a few of us just stared at the food. Someone uttered a few Tigrinya words of dismay, and we all looked at him. Realizing that we were all Eritreans (at least we all spoke Tigrinya), we got up and sat together at some distance from the others. We exchanged our names and started to get to know each other. We all nodded in unison when someone mentioned Tesfaye. We all were indeed going to the same place, with a common human smuggler: Tesfaye.

Our group of comrades included Netsanet, Kubrom, Fitsum Gebretateos, Fitsum Gebrehiwet, Beidu, and an Ethiopian named Girmaye Kibret. Netsanet was a ten-year-old girl who was traveling to Kenya with us to reunite with her parents, who had immigrated to Kenya many years earlier. Kubrom was an interesting character. A man in his mid- to late thirties, he was the oldest among us. We were from the same neighborhood—he had lived in Asmara, near Bar Mariana, about five blocks from my home. I probably had passed by his house many times on the way to school. Kubrom told us that he had once before tried to leave Eritrea, through Sudan. He was caught by the members of the Ethiopian security and detained at the notorious St. Mary's high-security prison. With the help of his family members, and with a great deal of money, he was released after years of imprisonment. The time he spent in prison had so traumatized Kubrom that he could abide no mention of our not making it to Kenya. If this trip now seemed like a do-or-die enterprise to *me*, it was all the more so for Kubrom.

Fitsum Gebretateos was a slim, light-complexioned, and ever-smiling young man who assumed the de facto leadership role in our group. Even though Fitsum had spent many years in Addis Ababa working as a mechanic and as a truck driver's assistant, when he spoke Tigrinya he sounded as if he had never left Eritrea. Fitsum was very quiet and very observant. But once you earned his trust, you could see his real personality: witty, sharp, and very funny.

Another member of our group was Fitsum Gebrehiwet. Fitsum Gebrehiwet was native to Eritrea—or said that he was, yet he was no master of the Tigrinya language. He claimed to have been born and raised in Dekemhare, Eritrea, and to have lived in Addis Ababa for a few years. Yet I doubted this and, for better or worse, I took him to be someone from the northern part of Ethiopia who was impersonating an Eritrean. Fitsum Gebrehiwet mentioned in a conversation that he used to drive a truck. I used the opportunity to challenge him to prove that he could actually drive a truck by showing us his driver's license. Without any hesitation, he took out his Ethiopian government-issued driving license and handed it to me. I examined the license thoroughly then gave it back without commenting on it. Based on what I saw on the license, he appeared to be who he said he was. Later on, when we got to

Kenya, I confessed to him and to the group that I'd suspected him of really being from northern Ethiopia and had asked to see his driver's license in order to verify his birthplace. I suggested diplomatically that he needed to do better with his Tigrinya if he was to claim that he grew up in Eritrea, let alone in Dekemhare. In this way, in the early days of our journey, I had been attempting to check out the type of company we were traveling with.

Beidu was a quiet, calm, and intelligent young man. As he would prove more than once during our trip, he had the highest academic learning of all of us.

Girmaye Kibret was the only non-Eritrean in our company. He was an Ethiopian of the Amhara nationality. Since the Amhara people were ruling Ethiopia during that time, we did not know how to take his presence among us. We listened to his story. Girmaye said that he was a taxi driver in Addis Ababa. A few months earlier, though, he received a draft notice to join the Ethiopian army, and he was leaving his country instead of joining an army that was brutally suppressing its people. Even though we all listened to his story attentively, I am sure we all were half suspecting that, sooner or later, he was going to expose us and hand us over to the Ethiopian security agency. Because we did not trust him, we laughed and joked in his presence but left any serious matters for discussion at times when he was not with us.

When our travel arrangements were made with the human smuggler Tesfaye, we were given the impression that Lemlem, Eden, and I would be the only escapees on the trip. Yet now we found out that Tesfaye had quite a few other passengers who were fleeing the country.

Later that evening, we arrived in Dilla, and Tesfaye took us from the bus station to a nearby hotel. Unsure about the implications of what we had discovered about Tesfaye and our trip, and exhausted by the long day's bus ride, we all slept without uttering any further words to each other.

The next day, Tesfaye gathered all of us in the hotel where Lemlem, Eden, and I had stayed and introduced us to each other. We exchanged names as if we had not done so the day before. We ordered breakfast and ate, staring at each other but not speaking. Tesfaye broke the silence to tell us that he needed to travel ahead of us to Moyale—the border town between Ethiopia and Kenya—to ascertain the security situation; he had heard that people had recently been caught trying to cross the border there. Additionally, he said, he wanted to make sure that his partners at the next stop were ready with the necessary vehicles for our transport. He demanded that either Lemlem or Eden should go with him, as it would apparently be easier for us to have only one woman in the group when we later tried to cross the border.

We had bought clothes the day before, so as to look like native Borena, one of the tribes that occupied the southern part of Ethiopia on the route we would take to Kenya. Both Lemlem and Eden had covered their heads. The women were undoubtedly warmer and more comfortable than I was in a long-sleeved red shirt, ill-fitting trousers that covered barely half my legs, and rubber shoes that soon started to cut into my ankles with every step. With these country-style clothes, we managed to blend in with the stream of travelers along the southern route. I reflected on this twist of fate: almost nine years earlier we had worked hard to assimilate with the city folks in Asmara, and now we were dressing down in order to assimilate with the Ethiopian villagers.

Tesfaye and Eden set out later that afternoon, and the rest of us were left in limbo. Internally, I was in turmoil. Eden, my brother's intended wife, had just departed to a place I had never heard of, with a man I had met only a few days before.

That afternoon at around six, Lemlem, Kubrom, and I made the unusual decision to go to the hotel bar. When the waitress came to serve us, Kubrom ordered a beer and I ordered a double shot of cognac, straight up. Lemlem could not believe her ears when I placed my order. She stared at me and told me to stop it. I told her to mind her own business. I guess when she saw my face she realized there was nothing she could do, so she sat there in stone-faced silence.

Lemlem knew that even with all the access I'd had to alcohol at home and outside our house, I had avoided drinking. At a younger age, thanks to my family's liberal view on many things, I had tasted beer, whiskey, and cognac, and hated both the taste and smell of each. Yet when the waitress came back with Kubrom's beer and my cognac, Kubrom had only a sip from his beer while I took the cognac in one gulp. I ordered another one. Lemlem just sat there, sipping lemonade and watching me.

Eden's sudden and unexpected departure from us signaled to me that we had reached a point of no return in our journey. There would not be any turning back. From that day on, it was do or die. I worried throughout the night: What I had done in letting her go? I thought of all the things that could go wrong. Every possibility that came to mind was scary.

I did not know whether my companions also drank to numb their nerves. But I tried to escape my worries that night, thinking that the cognac would knock me out. But drinking was not able to relieve me of the guilt and pain that consumed me. No amount of alcohol could have overcome my feelings of utter helplessness and loss of control. As a cocky teenager, I had been so sure about most things in life before that day, but no more. I cried bitterly underneath the blankets. I just kept asking myself, what the hell was I thinking to let her go? I felt like it had to have been the right decision, because I had little choice in the matter. Yet, moments later, the doubt would set in again and I feared I had committed a terrible crime. Still, I had no idea what that crime was. I was very confused.

The next day all of us got together for breakfast. After we started talking among ourselves, it was evident that Tesfaye had led each of us to believe that we would be the only ones on the trip. We now saw that there were a total of nine of us, all together, fleeing Ethiopia, including a ten-year-old girl. My sister, my sister-in-law-to-be, and I were the only ones going as a group.

On Monday, October 2, Lemlem and I left the market town of Dilla and boarded a bus with Tesfaye to Yirga Cheffe, arriving about two hours later. On Tuesday, October 3, we departed from Yirga Cheffe at six a.m. and arrived at our next destination, Hagere Maryam, at nine a.m.

The southern Ethiopian town of Hagere Maryam was infested with Ethiopian security services. I was shocked by the density of security forces in the area. It was easy to differentiate them from the villagers—the security agents had shiny shoes, their skin texture was smoother, and they invariably dressed in khaki. In another effort to blend in, I bought a bag of *khat*, a narcotic green plant, and walked around as if I were a khat merchant.

I was terrified of us getting caught. My fear turned into an outburst when Tesfaye gathered us all into a room. In the middle of our discussion, Tesfaye mentioned that we might have to stay in Hagere Maryam for the rest of the week. When I heard that, I lost my temper and told Tesfaye either he or I would make it alive to Nairobi—but definitely not both of us. The two Fitsums grabbed me by the arm and took me outside so we could talk in private. Once we left the room, I started explaining to them how dangerous the place was and there was no chance of us staying in that town for a week without getting caught by the Ethiopian security agents. They told me we should do whatever we could to leave Hagere Maryam as soon as we could, but my actions were not helpful. Blame it on youth or innocence—I did not agree with them at the time, but at least I promised to keep my mouth shut until we left Hagere Maryam.

Two days later, on Thursday, October 5, we left Hagere Maryam on a truck headed for the next town, Yabello, where we were told there would be a checkpoint. We approached Yabello around six p.m. The plan was to skirt around the checkpoint on foot, through the jungle. My legs started to hurt because of the rubber shoes that chafed against my ankles, causing them to swell and bleed. We were able to cross the checkpoint through the bushes without incident and went about the main street in Yabello, looking for our next connection.

We found a trailer to take us around nine in the evening and were able to get a ride to Mega, the next town. We trekked through the jungle to cross the checkpoint entering the town of Mega and boarded the same truck, which was waiting for us a few kilometers away from the checkpoint. After riding for a few hours, we came close to the checkpoint to enter the border town of Moyale. It was Friday, October 6, 1989. The truck stopped before reaching the checkpoint around two a.m. and waited there till dawn.

At around five thirty a.m., we heard a loud commotion in a house across the street. The soldiers on duty rushed to the house and left the checkpoint unattended. We looked at each other, unbelieving, then slowly walked through the checkpoint to Moyale without anyone asking us for ID. We later found out that a husband had come home and caught his wife with another man in the house; the men had started fighting. The soldiers had responded to the wife's call for help.

Once we crossed the Moyale checkpoint, we walked across the town and into Moyale through a river that divides both the town and the countries.

We had made it to Kenya. It was six a.m., and Tesfaye took us to a coffee shop, where we had breakfast. At the coffee shop, Tesfaye left us and came back with Eden. It was a great relief to finally see her.

Eden and Tesfaye had traveled to Moyale with Tesfaye's friend who owned a truck. After driving for most of the day, they arrived in Moyale and Tesfaye left Eden with a family that were related to him by marriage. Eden was extremely appreciative to the family for their hospitality and great treatment during her stay.

Afterward, Tesfaye pointed us to a clothing shop and told us to meet back there at dark. In the meantime, he said, we should be careful to avoid suspicion from both Ethiopian and Kenyan security agents. He advised us to split up and to blend in with the townspeople as much as we could. In other words, we were on our own.

But by noon, all of us had walked through the entirety of the tiny town of Moyale several times and were finding it impossible to avoid each other. Finally, a group of us led by Fitsum Gebretateos decided to cross back to the Ethiopian side of town and spend a few hours there, where it would take less effort for us to blend in, and wait to return until closer to the time we were to meet Tesfaye. At around eight that evening, we all made it to the shop where Tesfaye had told us to meet. After a few minutes of polite but tired conversation, we dropped to the floor for a few hours of sleep.

In the middle of the night, we were startled awake by a sudden banging, shouting, and screaming. Three armed men forced open the door of the shop and started kicking us awake, claiming to be Kenyan security officers. They shouted at us to get up to go to the police station. We huddled together in a corner of the shop, terrified.

Tesfaye burst from the other room and started yelling that the men were from the Central Investigation Department. "Give them whatever you have! These are CID… they will arrest us!" he shouted. With these words, we understood then that it was actually a robbery. We would have to give these "security officials" our money if we were to get away with our lives. Tesfaye motioned to us to turn over whatever we had, and we obliged. I handed over what was left of the 450 Ethiopian birr I had started out with, and the rest of our group did the same. Kubrom was hurt the most; he had close to five thousand birr and was forced to give them all of it.

Little did we know that this would be just the beginning of a night full of ordeal.

After the men had stomped out with our money and any of our worldly belongings that had value, we stood shaking in the dark shop, listening to the sounds of their truck peeling away. Tesfaye led us out of the shop and, under cover of the darkness, took us to a graveyard on the outskirts of town. We took refuge in the tombs. To make matters worse, Mother Nature started to bless us with her rain at that moment. The rain that we hoped would be a drizzle turned into a thunderstorm. We got soaked, and the darkness was complete. Under those conditions, there was nowhere we could go. I held Lemlem's hand tightly.

Our bodies started shaking from the cold and shock, yet we were so terrified of being caught that we had to keep our teeth clenched together to keep them from chattering; we could not allow ourselves to make any sound. Whenever we heard a sound or detected motion, we would stare in that direction, even though we could see nothing but dark. It felt, that night, like we faced death eye to eye. Now I truly understood why armies did everything they could to avoid waging war during the rainy season. The only positive aspect of that night was that the moon did not come out until the early morning hours. Although we could see nothing, at least we had the security of knowing we could not be seen. We rested as best we could, cold, wet, and afraid.

Tesfaye took us to a coffee shop in Moyale the next morning. After he bought us breakfast, we left the Kenyan side of the town and went back to the Ethiopian side, yet again, to search for another safer route to cross to Kenya.

We boarded a truck and started following the alternate route from Moyale to Hidilola. Around noon, we arrived at one of the small villages in the Hidilola district, yet another Ethiopian town along the Kenyan border with a very small population. We hid in the bush for the remainder of the day.

From that moment on, by day we were continually on alert for the movements of Ethiopian and Kenyan security forces, and by night we were in the bush, waking up with every sound, real or imagined.

After walking for about forty kilometers up and down the Werda Mountain, we arrived in Sololo, Kenya, at six a.m. Sunday morning. Tesfaye took us to a hut where we met a young man named Ibrahim, whom Tesfaye introduced to us as his partner. The family prepared a breakfast for us: it was a sort of porridge, a gruel made by boiling corn meal flour in water. We later learned that the name of our first meal in Kenya was *ugali*.

We ate gratefully and thanked the family, and Tesfaye and his partner Ibrahim led us back to the bush to hide ourselves for the rest of the day.

My ankle was getting worse, and by this time a mix of blood and pus had started to drip from it. Exhausted by what had obviously become an infection, I lay down to sleep on the ground next to Lemlem and Eden. When I woke up, it was three in the afternoon and the Kenyan sun was already hanging low in the sky. I felt moisture on my hands and asked Lemlem and Eden where it had come from. They told me I had slept through a heavy rain in the morning and a burning sun that had come out in the afternoon. My clothes had been soaked but had had time to dry completely. I felt better, though, from the long rest, and we left Sololo and continued our journey to Marsabit on a truck around four in the afternoon.

Once we left the forest and boarded the truck, we could easily see the lions, giraffes, and zebras roaming around our hiding place. Somehow either the wild animals were avoiding us—concerned for their safety, mistaking us for hunters—or we had sheer luck on our side, but we were able to get safely out of the Sololo forest.

We arrived at Marsabit the next day, Monday, October 9, 1989. Marsabit is about 170 kilometers south of Sololo and about 530 kilometers north of Nairobi, Kenya's capital. The roughness of the road had made our ride to Marsabit excruciating. Every time the truck hit a bump, our bodies were slammed against the back of the truck. The high speed at which the truck traveled jerked us up and down. And there were plenty of potholes! It felt like the truck was going to fall apart. But we got there at last. We stayed the rest of the afternoon on the outskirts of the town. In the evening, Tesfaye took three of us to one hotel, another three to another hotel, and then he took Lemlem, Eden, and Netsanet to spend the night with a Kenyan family he knew.

I boarded with Fitsum Gebretateos and Fitsum Gebrehiwet. Not long after we had checked into the hotel and the three of us had taken welcome showers, a knock came at the door. Were we caught? Could we just ignore the knock? We had made it all the way into Kenya without being discovered, but our safety wasn't guaranteed. I was scared I would be shipped back to Asmara, and what then? Would I go to prison?

Another knock came at the door, and I realized we had no choice. I opened it thinking it was Tesfaye. Instead, a man in a gray suit and a red tie stood in the doorway. From behind him, two men in civilian clothes emerged. They all came into the room and demanded to see our passports. We were not sure how to respond to yet another ambush. We were not sure whether these were more people sent by Tesfaye or truly Kenyan security officers. But then, why would Tesfaye send these people knowing we did not have a single penny in our pockets? We looked at one another, each hoping someone else would provide a response. But what each saw was a face with as much concern and confusion as their own. We just kept staring at each other.

When we failed to produce any documents, we were rounded up and led to the police station. We were booked for illegally entering Kenya.

There, we handed over everything we had left, everything that had survived the first shakedown. In my case, the only thing I still had was my notebook, and I handed it over to the officer in charge. Tuesday, October 10, 1989, was the last day I scribbled in my notebook.

When the police officer led us to a jail cell in the police station, we found our friends Kubrom, Beidu, and Girmaye Kibret waiting there, already in custody. At that point, there was nothing left to do but worry about the fate of Lemlem, Eden, and Netsanet.

It was dark in the cell at Marsabit police station. We all sat in silent misery, a two-by-four-meter cage crowding us together so all we could do was stare at each other. I wanted to pray for Lemlem, Eden, and Netsanet. The problem was I did not know what to pray for. Should I ask God to bring them to us? Or should I ask God to help them get to Nairobi safely? Before I could finish formulating these thoughts, Tesfaye, the human smuggler, was thrown into the cell with us. We all stared at him, but no one said a word. At this point, we had a clear understanding of Tesfaye's capabilities. We were sure he had something to do with us ending up in prison.

The next day when the police officers woke us up to eat breakfast, I looked up and happened to see Lemlem, Eden, and Netsanet down the hall, standing single file next to a desk where a police officer sat, writing. Lemlem turned to stare at me. While the police officer had his head down, I gestured to Lemlem that she should not show any sign of recognizing us. I waved her away, as if to say, "Go!" and that they should be on their own.

With that, Lemlem, Eden, and Netsanet were accepted as asylum seekers, because the family they spent the night with had advised them to go to the police station—something we did not even know we could have done! The family in fact brought the three of them to the police station.

The rest of us remained in jail.

About three days later, Tesfaye was released. We did not know why he had been detained with us, and we did not know why he was being released.

As we learned later, after he got released, Tesfaye went back to Addis Ababa and asked Aya Mohammed Kelifa for money in order to get us out of the Kenyan jail. Aya Mohammed refused to pay the ransom money and called other friends and family in Kenya instead to try to help us.

Although we were treated fairly well, there were other significant challenges at the jail. Bedbugs and head and body lice became our nemesis for a while. Initially, we saw them crawling along the walls. But of course, not long after, they were crawling on our bodies and through our hair.

Also, because the wound on my ankle, caused by the rubber shoes I had worn since departing from Hagere Maryam, was daily getting worse, the police officers allowed me to sleep outside the cell for the first few days. When my ankle was bleeding more or less continuously, one of the officers took me to a nearby clinic. There, while I was waiting in line, I asked the officer if I could use the restroom. In the restroom, I picked up a piece of paper towel, hoping I could get a message to Lemlem and Eden. Then I went back to the line.

When it was my turn, I was led into the clinic. The nurse on duty examined the bleeding on my ankle then got up and went to another room. My ankle was in awful shape. The cut was much deeper than I had realized. Adrenaline was keeping me going. I thought that maybe I would lose my foot. The cut had been open a long time, and amputation wasn't uncommon. But I couldn't do anything other than wait for the nurse, so I took that opportunity to scribble "from Dawit" on the piece of paper towel in Tigrinya, and I put it around the fifty-dollar bill and hid it again.

The nurse came back and cleaned and treated the wound and gave the police a written order for me to come back the next day. On the way back to the police station, I spotted Lemlem and Eden standing by the side of the road, watching me from a distance. As we passed them, I casually dropped the paper I had been holding, concealed in my palm, and signaled to Lemlem and Eden to pick it up.

The next day, the two women showed up at the jail with a large container of spaghetti for us. We all salivated at the smell of the familiar food.

Despite the geographical closeness of Eritrea and Kenya, the two countries are culturally two different planets. We had a hard time adapting to the traditional Kenyan food served at the jail. We were always served *chai na mandazi* for breakfast and *ugali na sukuma wiki* for lunch and again for dinner. Chai is tea with milk, and *mandazi* is fried sweet bread—like a doughnut. The *mandazi* we got in prison were soaked with oil, which we found impossible to eat at five in the morning. So the spaghetti was like manna from heaven for us! We ate the pasta to the last morsel.

Later on, Lemlem and Eden told us they had found the fifty-dollar bill wrapped in the piece of paper towel I dropped for them—the money from Biniam's aunt, which I had been so reluctant to take from her on our way out of Addis Ababa; the errand had felt like an unnecessary burden and I had resented it. I had carried that bill secured on my person throughout the ups and downs of our journey, protecting it from thieves and even from our associates. When I threw it to them, I had been thinking it was likely the last time I would see them. They exchanged the fifty dollars for one thousand Kenyan shillings and fed us all.

A couple of weeks later, a man named Aboy Araya Weldehiwet arrived in Marsabit. Aya Mohammed had called Aboy Araya Weldehiwet and informed him that his old friend's children were stranded in Marsabit, a town 530 kilometers from Nairobi, a destination that requires more than twelve hours by bus.

The same day that Aboy Araya received the call asking to come get me out of prison, he was told that both of his fuel tanker trucks had gotten into accidents, one on its way to Mombasa and the other on the way to Kampala, Uganda. Aboy Araya asked his friends to handle the loss of his vital business properties and decided to come to Marsabit himself, a job he felt could only be done by him. To Aboy Araya, saving and looking after his old friend's kids was the most important thing for him at that moment.

Aboy Araya had come to rescue us.

AN ORDINARY MAN WITH AN EXTRAORDINARY HEART

"It is under the greatest adversity that there exists the greatest potential for doing good, both for oneself and others." —Dalai Lama XIV

When I first saw Aboy Araya Weldehiwet through the small window in the cell door, I was not sure what to make of him. The man I had imagined—based on the stories I'd been told by my dad—was a wealthy Eritrean merchant. But the person standing at the desk at the entrance of the police station looked somewhat less than affluent.

I studied him carefully. Aboy Araya was about five feet, nine inches (173 centimeters) tall and weighed about 120 pounds (fifty-five kilograms). He had a curly Afro that covered most of his forehead. He rested his hands on top of the desk, which was level with his chest. He wore a worn-out light yellow jacket over a striped shirt.

This, I thought, could not possibly be my dad's good friend. This man cannot possibly be the hero who is going to get us out of this jail! No way!

After talking to the police officers for a few minutes, the man turned and walked out of the police station. Deciding that his appearance at the jail had nothing to do with us, I put him out of my mind.

In his travels for the ELF, my dad met Aboy Araya Weldehiwet, who lived in Adi-Tsunu'ay, the village bordering Adi-Hayo on the northwest tip of the village. Aboy Araya was returning from purchasing cattle from Areza, one of the marketplaces in the southern part of Eritrea.

Aboy Araya Weldehiwet was born to his father, Aboy Weldehiwet Gebremichael, and his mother, Adey Dehab Teclemariam, in Adi-Tsunu'ay. Aboy Araya's date of birth is determined by associating the time frame with a widely known event that took place at the time—he was born around the time the British arrived in Eritrea, circa 1941–42. He was a hardworking farmer from the town of Adi-Tsunu'ay and not political. He was born under British rule, but he married Adey Leterbrhan Fsehaye from Zawl, who was born in 1952 under the federated Ethiopian regime.

With a growing family, Aboy Araya left Adi-Tsunu'ay in 1967 and went to Asmara to find a better income. Initially, Aboy Araya worked at multiple small auto body repair shops, including with the Haji-Hasen family, who owned a well-known auto shop in Asmara. He lived there for almost ten years, but in 1975, when it became extremely difficult and dangerous to live in Asmara, Aboy Araya left the capital and went back to Adi-Tsunu'ay. He tried to get into the produce business using his farmland, but the violence in the area—in fact in all of Eritrea—was unbearable. It was difficult for civilians to move from one village to another, which made selling his crops impossible.

In 1978, Aboy Araya left Eritrea and went to Sudan, eventually settling in Nairobi, Kenya.

By the time Aboy Araya arrived at the jail where I was held, the immigration office in Marsabit, Kenya, had accepted the asylum petitions of Lemlem, Eden, and ten-year-old Netsanet. A few days later, the immigration office transferred them with a group of other asylum seekers in Marsabit to a refugee camp in Thika, a small town on the outskirts of Nairobi.

The rest of us were praying through the hours for our release. Kubrom, Fitsum Gebretateos, Fitsum Gebrehiwet, Beidu, Girmaye Kibret, and I were tormented by both hope and despair. On one hand, we were hopeful that we would be granted political asylum. On the other hand, we were concerned by the alternative: a court could reject our petition and hand us over to the Ethiopian security forces, who would in turn put us in one of two maximum-security prisons—the infamous Ethiopian prison in Addis Ababa commonly referred as Alem Bekagn ("farewell to the world" in Amharic) or the torture chambers of the infamous Maryam Gmb (St. Mary's walls) in Asmara.

After about three weeks in the jail, we were told our case would go to court in three days. Our cell was quieter than normal for those three days. We started counting down at seventy-two hours. Yet on our trial date, for some technical reason we did not understand at the time, we were transferred to the Marsabit district detention center. To say that we were traumatized when we arrived and saw the huge prison hall would be an understatement. The six of us were deposited—by ourselves—in a prison hall that could have held a thousand people. We huddled together in a corner, shocked into silence, and stared around the huge garrison. The wall on the other side of the room was too far away for us to see. The guards brought us dinner, but we barely touched it. When the door closed on us, we were in near total darkness.

It would be the longest, darkest, and scariest night of my life. In comparison, spending the night in that cage seemed worse than getting robbed in the middle of the night, spending sleepless nights in graveyards, and passing through long stretches of mountains under the cover of night.

But they say that it's always darkest before the dawn. The day of our asylum trial arrived after the darkest and most dreadful night.

The next day we were taken to court at nine in the morning. The judge rendered his verdict quickly, informing us of our two options: pay ten thousand Kenyan shillings total for the group (roughly five hundred dollars US) or spend the next six months in prison. We gasped. None of us was in possession of that kind of a sum after being robbed more than once on the long journey. We looked at each other despairingly.

Then Aboy Araya Weldehiwet stepped forward out of the crowd. It was indeed the supposedly undistinguished gentleman I had seen at the jail a few days earlier. Aboy Araya turned to us. He instructed us to plead guilty for crossing the Kenyan border illegally and to accept the fine. Through our translator, we complied. Aboy Araya paid the ten thousand Kenyan shillings on our behalf.

After we had signed the necessary documents, the court released us back into the custody of the police. We were told that on that night we would have to sleep outside the police station with the other asylum seekers waiting for interview. We were taken to immigration headquarters to start the asylum application process the following morning.

Covered only with thin blankets provided by the station chief, we lay down on the ground outside the police station. Yet, despite the ludicrousness of the situation, the deep sleep of that first night of freedom helped us begin to forget the previous weeks' nightmares.

I was able to get to know Aboy Araya during the two days he stayed with us in Marsabit. He gave me his phone number and told me to call him once we arrived in Nairobi. He bought me clothes and gave me three thousand Kenyan shillings for my meals and personal expenses during my stay in Marsabit. Aboy Araya left Marsabit with the nine p.m. bus to Nairobi.

Our interviews for political asylum with the Central Investigation Department of Marsabit district began a week later.

"*Najua Kiswahili?*" was the first question the Kenyan head of the Marsabit district CID asked me during my interview. "Do you speak Kiswahili?"

Kiswahili is a common language heavily used across the central and eastern African countries. "*Sijui, mzee* (I don't know, sir)," I responded, using the few Kiswahili words and phrases I had learned during my weeks in Kenya.

I had learned that *mzee* meant "sir." Later on that knowledge was deepened into an understanding that the term was used to address any older man, an elder, rather than being a formal title, as in the British court. As for the word *sijui*, I had all too quickly learned how to say "I don't know" in the Kiswahili-speaking border towns between Ethiopia and Kenya. *Sijui* had been my very good friend for some time.

"Do you speak English?" continued the inquisitor.

"A little bit" was all I knew to say. I immediately regretted how little vocabulary I had retained from the many English-language classics I had read at the British Council Library in Asmara.

"What is your name?" continued the head of the CID.

I knew enough English to understand the questions being asked. My response was short and to the point: "Dawit Gebremichael Habte."

"Is that like David?" he asked, starting to put his pen to his notebook.

"No, sir," I protested. "Dawit, not David." For some reason I felt upset and irritated.

Those feelings must have sounded in my tone, for the CID man stopped and looked up at me. I stared back and started spelling my three names: my given name, my father's first name, and my grandfather's first name. He continued to look at me without saying a word. He could not have had a clue as to what was going through my mind. I wondered if he had any idea how dehumanizing it felt for me to have to seek asylum. I had a place I called home. I had people I called family. I had left behind caring and thoughtful friends and neighbors. And now I was stuck in a place I didn't even know what to call. I had spent weeks in prison, and if all that wasn't enough, now someone was trying to bastardize the only thing I still possessed and considered to be solely mine—my name.

At the time of this asylum interview in Marsabit, it had been exactly fifty-six days since the commencement of my journey into uncertainty, into exile. I was only fifteen years old. In less than two months, I had seen a prototype of what life had to offer once people left home. I had traversed through several spectra of life previously unknown to me and had experienced a lot of firsts. For the first time I had boarded an airplane. For the first time I had spent nights in bushes and graveyards. For the first time I had gone without food for three consecutive days. For the first time I had eaten *ugali* (a stiff porridge made from corn flour mixed with boiled vegetable soup). For the first time I'd had close encounters with wild animals—his highness the king of the jungle (lion), zebra, giraffe, and, of course, the sneaky snake. For the first time I had been in prison. For the first time I had crossed the borders of multiple nations illegally and become an "illegal alien." And, for yet another first, I was being interviewed to determine my fitness and desirability to remain in Kenya. All this happened in fewer than sixty days since I left home, where I had been fortunate to barely know or care where my daily bread came from. Though I knew I should have been grateful to have finally arrived at this point, I felt humiliated by the process.

It took about two weeks for our application for political asylum to be approved, and we had to stay in the Marsabit police station the whole time. Afterward, our case was transferred to the refugee camp at Thika. It was time to leave Marsabit for good. No more sleeping on the ground outside the police station. We were embarking on yet another voyage to an as yet unknown destination. All we knew was the name Thika.

At around eight p.m. on a cold night, more than twenty of us who were seeking asylum boarded a truck to go to Thika, a distance of almost five hundred kilometers. It did not take long before we started bouncing like soccer balls every time the truck hit a huge bump on the gravel road. The distance we traveled that cold and painful night could easily have been a thousand kilometers. We finally arrived at Thika the next day.

I stayed in the refugee camp in Thika for a few days, listening and learning, conferring with other refugees. Then early one morning I sneaked out with other veterans and took a minibus to Nairobi, ending up in the district called Eastleigh, in the eastern part of Nairobi. As Aboy Araya instructed me to do after leaving the camp, I called him from a coffee shop and told him my location. He walked through the door a few minutes later and took me to his house. There, I found Lemlem and Eden.

After about a month and a half in Nairobi, I was picking up Kiswahili, so I asked Aboy Araya if I could work in his

An Ordinary Man

matatu, a minibus used as a taxicab. Teweldebrhan, Aboy Araya's brother-in-law, was driving the matatu.

The witty and humorous Teweldebrhan joined the Eritrean Liberation Front at a young age to fight for his country's independence. Like me, anyone could easily see the pain Teweldebrhan felt in his current unpredictable refugee life. He had a wife, a family, a country. He lost everything because of the war, but he never lost his humor.

The Arabic word *maalesh* ("never mind" or "sorry") and the Tigrinya phrase *shelel belo* ("let it go") were some of Teweldebrhan's favorite expressions and would trigger an elongated explanation of his days as a freedom fighter. Whenever I or someone told Teweldebrhan, "Maalesh, Teweldino," Teweldebrhan would respond by saying, "Listen, don't tell me maalesh. Maalesh is what took down our ELF." Teweldebrhan would not stop talking about the ELF and his comrades once the subject of Eritrean armed struggle was raised. He would passionately recount the battles he fought in various parts of Eritrea.

Initially, Aboy Araya was surprised when I asked him to work with Teweldebrhan in the matatu, and he told me I should not feel obligated to do that. I replied that I was not feeling any pressure by staying in his house at all. I just wanted to work and get to know the city. With that understanding, Aboy Araya let me start working for him. Some of the first few Kiswahili words I mastered included:

Jambo—What's up?
Habari (Habari yako)—What's new (What's new with you, how are you)?

Nzuri (Nzuri sanna)—Well (very well)

Twende—Let's go

Asante (Asante sanna)—Thanks (Thanks a lot)

Lete (Lete piesa)—Give me (Give me money)

Shawri yako—None of your business

Ngapi—How much (How many)

Sifuri, moja, mbili, tatu, nne, tano, sita, saba, nane, tti-sa, kumi, kumina-moja...—zero, one, two, three, four, five, six, seven, eight, nine, ten, eleven...

I usually spent most of my Sundays reading the *Daily Nation* and the *Standard* newspapers for Aboy Araya, both of which were written in English. Aboy Araya insisted that I read and translate for him the news detailed in the Kenyan papers. I tried to translate each news item from English to Tigrinya paragraph by paragraph. It was very challenging and frustrating at times to translate the news items, but I am sure it was a great opportunity for Aboy Araya and me to talk about the Eritrean armed struggle, among other things.

One Sunday, after my usual reading of the *Daily Nation*, I started to talk with Aboy Araya. Usually he was the one asking questions once I finished going over the weekly news stories, but this time I wanted to ask him how and where he met my dad and how they became friends. All I heard from my dad was that they'd met on their way back from the marketplace in Areza, a town in the southern part of Eritrea.

"So, Aboy Araya. How did you and my dad meet?"

"Well, you see Dawitey"—Aboy Araya never called me Dawit, always referring to me as Dawitey, meaning "my Dawit"—"your dad and I met for the first time when we both were coming back from Areza in 1977. At the time, I'd gathered every penny I had saved by selling vegetables I planted in our farmland in Adi-Tsunu'ay and gone to Areza to purchase some cattle. I spent every penny I had to purchase three oxen from the cattle market in Areza. My plan was to take the cattle to Asmara and sell them there. I could then use the money I saved and the profit I made to rent an auto body repair shop in Asmara. Unfortunately, things usually did not go as we planned during those days. Asmara was surrounded by both Eritrean liberation movements, and there was no way for me to take my cattle to the city. I was not even able to take them to my village. Since your dad was a member of the ELF mass organization, he said he would keep my cattle in Adi-Hayo for a few days and help me take them to Asmara by the weekend. True to his word, your dad helped me take the three oxen to Asmara, and I was able to sell them there for a great deal of profit. But there were no possibilities to proceed with the rest of my plans. I went back to my village, and about a year later, during the summer of 1978, I left Eritrea and went to Sudan. I then came to Kenya after traveling through Juba in southern Sudan and Kampala in Uganda. It took me about three months to get to Nairobi from Khartoum, Sudan. I applied for refugee status in Kenya and I was granted a work permit and permanent residence."

A matatu has about twenty-four seats. Each matatu has a unique name and usually works a specific route. Between three and four people work in one matatu: a driver, a machine man, a conductor, and a *makanga* (doorkeeper). I started as a machine man while Teweldebrhan was the driver of the matatu called Africa Songa Mbele (Africa March Forward). The sole responsibility of a machine man is to count the number of passengers boarding the minibus. At the end of the day, the number counted is multiplied by the fare, and the conductor is required to hand over that much money. I loved the adventurous nature of the work. I was getting paid to tour the entire city—a great job I do not think any fifteen-year-old would turn down.

But it was hard work. Teweldebrhan and I had to wake up at four thirty a.m. to get to the garage, and our shift started at five a.m. It did not end till midnight. It took me quite a while to get used to these hours. But, as I would discover, if you put your mind to something, nothing is impossible.

So, Africa Songa Mbele became my regular Monday–Friday job in Nairobi.

For the matatu crew, breakfast is taken from ten to eleven a.m., lunch from two to three p.m., and dinner from approximately seven to eight p.m. Drivers usually eat their breakfast and dinner at either end of the route. For lunch break, however, the drivers actually get off the minibus, and another one is hired for about two hours. When the machine man takes a lunch break, he hands the machine to the driver for a single route, and the driver monitors the passenger count. The conductor and the makanga have to take their lunches by turns. When the conductor is on lunch break, the makanga collects the money while watching the door, and they reverse when the makanga takes his break.

After working as a machine man for about a month, I had picked up enough Kiswahili vocabulary that I was able to relieve the conductor. I gave the machine man's job to the driver. At the same time, I also started practicing jumping in and out of the matatu's door to learn the highly esteemed skills of a makanga.

Makanga is the most dangerous job I have ever faced in my life. A makanga stands by the open door of a matatu that's moving at eighty to ninety kilometers per hour, luring passengers to his matatu by yelling his guts out. When passengers are spotted by the side of the road, waving their arms, the makanga jumps out of the matatu while it is still moving at about thirty to forty kilometers per hour. Then, once the passengers are boarded, the makanga runs alongside the vehicle until it reaches a speed of forty to fifty kilometers per hour before he jumps back in.

On my first couple of days at work, I noticed, and admired, the neatness of Kenyan students. The boys dressed in black pants and jackets, white shirts, and black ties, while the girls dressed in blue skirts and jackets, white shirts, and blue bow ties. All of them had book bags, which only a few students carried back home. I was so impressed and realized that I desperately missed school. Watching the students going to school and returning home made me seriously consider doing some schoolwork on my own.

As a result, I decided to start reading high school math and English on the weekends. I borrowed Aboy Araya's eldest son's books whenever I got a chance. I also started buying novels from the traders selling used books in the streets of downtown Nairobi. After a few such purchases, I told the trader that I could not afford to spend my whole day's salary buying books. I asked him if there was a library in town. To my surprise, the man offered to let me return the books that I read and buy each new one for 10 to 15 percent of its original price. I accepted. From that time on, the man had a loyal customer, and I got to read a book for ten to fifteen shillings—peanuts compared to the one hundred or more Kenyan shillings he charged for a single book.

Some of the books I read while I was in Nairobi included Kenyan fiction about various tribes, Bill Cosby's *Love and Marriage*, Agatha Christie's novels, and high school textbooks (mainly math and physics).

After about five months in Nairobi, we received mail from my brother, Afewerki, with sponsorship documents for re-settlement to the United States. Afewerki had left Eritrea in the spring of 1985 after he was drafted to join the Ethiopian army. He then went to the United States through a refugee resettlement process sponsored by Ambassadors of Fourth Presbyterian Church, in collaboration with the International Office for Migration.

Our family resettlement process from Nairobi was also sponsored by the same Ambassadors of Fourth Presbyterian Church. We took our documents to the American Embassy in Nairobi, where we were informed that we would be called at some point for an interview.

After leaving the American Embassy to go back to work, I waved my hands to hail an incoming matatu, and when the driver saw me, he slowed down to about forty to fifty kilometers per hour. I grabbed the metal bar with my left hand, swerved to the right, and hopped on. I turned my face to the driver and said, "*Sarie moja* (one for free)," signaling that I actually worked for another matatu. The driver glanced back over his shoulder at me to confirm this. Our eyes locked. I felt an icy chill run through my body. The man I was staring at was Tesfaye, the human smuggler who had abandoned us in jail in Marsabit. I began to shake. What was I feeling then? Hard to say. There was so much I wanted to say to the man behind the wheel. Unfortunately, none of it was pleasant.

The moment stretched for what seemed like an eternity. It was as if, through some kind of telepathy, we were in a virtual parallel universe where there was just the two of us. It was he who finally broke eye contact. He turned his head and began to inch the matatu forward into traffic. He did not say a word. But I am sure his brain was processing as much information as mine. I imagined that he was wrestling with justifications for his misdeeds.

For my part, I was just stunned. I had no good memories of this man. I wanted to unload on him with all the anger and rage that was boiling in my head. I started choosing my words carefully. I also wanted to finish what I had started months ago, when I told this man that either he or I would make it to Nairobi alive—but not both of us. I wanted to deliver on my threat for the betrayal, for what we later learned he had done after he left us in the Kenyan jail, and more. This man had actually gone back to Addis Ababa and asked our family members for extra money to get us released from the Kenyan jail. Otherwise, according to Tesfaye, we were going to get deported to Ethiopia and would end up in prison. Luckily Aboy

Araya Weldehiwet informed Mohammed Kelifa, who was in Addis Ababa, not to pay and that he would handle the situation himself.

The minibus then stopped to pick up more passengers. Tesfaye had to look back to count the number of people boarding. But I was between him and the door. He had to face me.

I don't know what came to me then. As he turned his head and our eyes met again, I felt pity. I could hardly believe it, but I felt sorry for him. In the moment I saw that he was no better off than me. He had become just another asylum seeker in exile.

Surprising even myself, I outstretched my hand and greeted him, calling him by his first name—and he did the same. We exchanged smiles. He knew who I was, and somehow that made me feel better.

Forgiveness is indeed a conversation away. However, the difference between forgiveness and forgetting is day and night. I will never forget this man's betrayal and duplicity. But, for a reason I never understood, I decided to move on with my life.

A few days after my encounter with Tesfaye, I finally was able to get a phone number for my cousin Biniam's aunt in Addis Ababa. One late Saturday afternoon, I called Biniam's aunt and explained to her the problems I'd faced on my way to Nairobi and that I had lost her son's phone number. I told her that I had used the money she gave me, but now I had the money to give to her son. She was so gracious and told me that she'd been praying for us after Biniam told her what had happened. During our conversations, I asked her if she would still have given me the money to take to her son had she known I was crossing the border on foot. She said yes. She was so worried about her son that she was willing to take the risk for a miniscule window of hope that she could help him. I found her son using the number she gave me later that evening, and I gave him 1,250 Kenyan shillings, the equivalent of the fifty dollars his mother gave me. I felt free and relieved.

One afternoon I was taking a lunch break in the neighborhood of Eastleigh when I heard someone calling my name from a distance. I looked back and I saw my friend Haile Thika with two Kenyan police officers holding him by his arms. I was a bit surprised to see Haile in Eastleigh, considering I was expecting him to be in the refugee camp in Thika (which was why we called him Haile Thika). He kept waving his hands toward me, smiling nervously. Knowing exactly what was happening, I smiled back at Haile and started walking toward him and the police officers.

Once I reached them, Haile told me that the police officers had brought him to Eastleigh when he told them he did not have money. By then, it had become widely known that if refugees from Eritrea, Ethiopia, or Somalia were caught by Kenyan police officers, the police would first ask the refugees for money. If the refugees claimed they did not have any money, then the officers would take them to quiet and isolated areas and go through the refugees' pockets and take whatever they found. If they confirmed that the refugees were actually telling them the truth and they did not find anything, then the police would bring them to Eastleigh—heavily populated by immigrants from the Horn of Africa—so the refugees could "borrow" payoff money from their respective countrymen. Haile, the two police officers, and I knew what they wanted.

I greeted the police officer who was grabbing Haile's right arm, and we moved a few strides away from Haile and the other police officer. I asked him how much he was asking for. By then, I had become well accustomed to the culture of corruption Kenya was plagued with. It was crystal clear that bribery and corruption were the way of life in Kenya. Thus, I was direct in my dealings with the police officer.

The police said five hundred shillings, and I started walking away from him. The police officer followed me and said, "*Kuja hapa rafiki yangu. Unaenda wapi?*" It meant, "Come here my friend, where are you going?" Suddenly I was his "friend." He waved his arm, telling me to come back.

I told him to go ahead and take Haile to the police station, and I would rather pay off his boss. He caught up with me and told me we could talk about it. I stopped and looked back at Haile, and I saw Haile's face changing colors in disbelief, thinking that I was going to walk out on him. He had no idea my negotiation skills with Kenyan police had developed beyond what I would have ever wanted. Thanks to working in the matatu, I had become a ruthless negotiator.

The policeman then asked how much I would give him. I stared at him and told him what he was saying was a nonstarter. He then said the only way to let my friend go was to give him and his friend one hundred shillings each. I looked at him and at the other police officer. The police officer who was standing next to Haile started wandering around, as if I had not seen him when he was looking at me to see how much I was going to give his friend. I looked back at the policeman standing next to me and told him I was going to give him and his friend forty shillings, and if he didn't want that, I had a business to take care of and I was not going to waste my time dealing with an unreasonable person. The policeman started throwing his hands up and down and acting confused. He said he could not believe what I just said, and how dare I insult him that way. The amazing part was that he was insulting himself when he dragged an innocent refugee to borrow ransom money. But that was the last thing on his mind. To him, it was business as usual.

Still acting as if I had insulted his mother by offering forty shillings, he said 150 shillings was the least he would take. I offered fifty shillings. After a few ups and downs and each of us threatening the other that he was going to walk away from the deal, we finally seemed to agree on eighty shillings. When I was almost certain that the policeman was going to take eighty shillings, I put four bills of twenty shillings in his pocket and told him I was going to walk away whether he took the money or not. In other words, I gave him an opportunity to deceive his friend, considering most of our negotiation was taking place at a distance from the other police officer. He made a signal to his colleague to let Haile go, and his friend's eyes were staring at his pocket to make sure he did not put his hands in it to take out some of the money I gave him.

Haile and I walked toward the coffee shop on Thirteenth Street to catch up. Such is the life of refugees awaiting resettlement wherever they might be, from Bosnia to Southeast Asia to West Africa. A refugee is always a pawn to be used.

Haile became a highly successful immigrant in the US. Shortly after his arrival, he took a good look at his options of working as a parking attendant in Washington, DC, and he was not happy with what he saw, so he made a courageous decision to go to a university in Omaha, Nebraska. For an African immigrant who arrived in the Washington, DC, area, Omaha is a place in the middle of nowhere. At age thirty-three, Haile earned a BS in aeronautical engineering and later a graduate degree in aviation business administration from the University of Nebraska.

In Nairobi there was a vibrant Eritrean community organized by the local chapter of the National Union of Eritrean Women, one of the many EPLF organizations. Lemlem, Eden, and I became active members, attending the organization's seminars and political education every Saturday.

When the number of youth joining the organization grew, we branched out to form a youth chapter. The youth chapter was led by a young lady and a young man who had lived in Kenya for most of their lives. During our political seminars, the two argued passionately on the issues they perceived would face post-independence Eritrea. Both were well read and, unfortunately, at first many of the topics they raised were beyond our comprehension.

We were overwhelmed by the information related to governance and the democratic process they were trying to instill in us. They dealt heavily with the types and structures of governance, parliamentary procedures, and electoral processes that post-independence Eritrea would need to adopt. One of them passionately defended the concept of a parliamentary government, and the other counterargued that presidential-based governance would be better. They lectured us about the three branches of government: executive, legislative, and judiciary.

I generally could not wait until the meetings and debates ended. But once they did, I immediately ran to the library shelves to read books about Eritrean history.

Via the various publications and documentaries produced by EPLF and foreign journalists, we learned about the brutal crimes the Ethiopian army was committing against the people of Eritrea. We read and saw footage of massacres committed at Ona, Basik Dira, Agordat, Hazemo, Hirgigo, Um Hajer, Woki-duba, Asmara, Shieeb, and other small villages in the western parts of Eritrea. No Eritrean ethnic group was spared from the Ethiopian death squads. All ages and all religions were targeted. In the village of Ona, for example, Ethiopian soldiers with machine guns rounded up the inhabitants at the village mosque and massacred more than six hundred innocent civilians. This cold-blooded butchery was ostensibly undertaken to avenge the death of their commanding general, who had been ambushed in November 1970 by the Eritrean freedom fighters.

The Ethiopian army's response to its losses of territory was brutal, ruthless, and indiscriminate. In her submission to the People's Tribunal in 1980, the British human rights activist

Mary Dines gave detailed accounts of the many genocides and war crimes committed by the Ethiopians:

> "On the morning of 13 March 1975, a group of three hundred Ethiopian soldiers on their way from Asmara to Keren passed through the village of Woki (population about twenty-five hundred) at seven a.m. They rounded up the villagers on a piece of wasted ground and shot thirty-seven dead. After this, most of the people fled into the hills, but the rest, believing there was nowhere safe to go, or that nothing else would happen, remained. On their return on March 14, the Ethiopians stopped again. They then proceeded to slaughter nearly five hundred people in the most gruesome way. Many women, children, and old men were bayoneted, and pregnant women were slit open. The Ethiopians then killed all the livestock and set fire to the houses. The slaughter was arbitrary and had no political connection with opposition forces. There are three mass graves outside the village."[27]

The massacre of innocent Eritreans at Keren by the Ethiopian military

27   Permanent People's Tribunal. *The Eritrean Case: Proceedings of the Permanent People's Tribunal of the International League for the Rights and Liberation of Peoples: Session on Eritrea. Milan, Italy, May 24–26, 1980.* "Ethiopian Repression of Eritrea," p. 309.

In 1988, at a town called Shieeb, more than four hundred women and children were run over by tanks to avenge the defeat of the Ethiopian army at Afabet. That was the nature of the Ethiopian colonization. The motto from the onset was clear: dry the sea to kill the fish.

Under the leadership of Stephanos, the representative of the EPLF mass organization's Nairobi branch, we did whatever we could to help the Eritrean revolutionaries. In addition to attending the political discussions every Saturday, we transcribed weekly news from the EPLF's shortwave radio program *Voice of the Masses*. Two members of our group, Sammy and Henock, had very good handwriting and they neatly rewrote our drafts. Then, on Sunday mornings, we made photocopies and sold the copies at the soccer field to the Eritrean residents of Nairobi. This way, we helped the people get up-to-date information on the Eritrean armed struggle.

My colleagues and I would transcribe the Voice of the Masses *radio broadcasts from this desk in Nairobi*

Meanwhile, Ethiopian mass atrocities in Eritrea were piling up. A few days after the port city of Massawa was liberated by the EPLF in February of 1990, the Ethiopians took their revenge by bombing the city with napalm and cluster bombs, weapons that had been banned by the United Nations. We saw a videotape of the Massawa war footage, which had been distributed by the EPLF Information Dissemination Division, at Aboy Tesfamariam and Adey Wubet's house in Westland, Nairobi. The Ethiopian army and its supporters had no qualms about pouring chemical agents on the civilians of Massawa, including striking the marketplace in the middle of the day, indiscriminately slaughtering women and children. Napalm sticks to human skin, causing severe burns, which we could see clearly in the videotape. The sight of young children and elders with pieces of their arms and legs blown off was horrific. Perhaps worst of all was that the video captured remnants of the bombs, which displayed "Made in USA" inscriptions. The documentary was clear evidence of the war crimes committed by the Ethiopian army, a clear demonstration of its mantra: dry the sea to kill the fish.

All of us burst into tears when we saw a kid painfully asking his older brother, "Are they going to bury us right away?" and the older brother, who could not have been older than six or seven years old, responding by saying, "No, we might be able to go to the hospital." As the Canadian documentary filmmaker Yvan Patry observed, the pain was indeed too much for the residents of Massawa. The pain of watching the documentary was too much for us as well. We were infuriated, but our resolve was hardened. We all pledged to increase our efforts to help the movement and to do our part to ease our people's pain and suffering. We decided to stage a variety show in commemoration of the liberated port of Massawa; the proceeds would be sent to support the work in the field.

Members of EPLF Youth Group – Kenya branch

We needed to form a band, and that we did. We called ourselves Arkb (catch-up). This name reflected our hope that we would grow to catch up with our idols in the revolution's cultural troops. Initially I was given two songs to work on, but once they heard my voice, I was assigned instead to help out with drums. Unfortunately, I was not cut out to be a drummer, either. But, since a revolution, particularly the Eritrean revolution, had a place for everyone, I was reassigned again, this time to help with choreography. Eden and I did very well with that. Lemlem, who had a beautiful, lilting voice, was assigned four songs.

As it turned out, our show caused quite a buzz among the Eritreans in Kenya. People came from all over the country to see us. Eritrean refugees came from the Thika refugee camp; some families came from as far as the Kenya–Uganda border town of Bungoma, traveling more than three hundred kilometers, and some traveled close to five hundred kilometers from the port town of Mombasa. The shining stars of the night were our coordinator, lead singer, and *krar* player, Habtom Debessai, our announcer, Abubaker Abdel'awel, lead guitarist, Nuredin, and vocalists Michael Fanuel and my sister Lemlem, with her song "Message of Love to the Parents From Their Children in the Trenches." My sister sang:

> *Parents, how dearly I miss you*
> > *always in my mind, constantly thinking of you*
> *it is painful thinking of you*
> > *our dear parents, I hope my greetings reach you*
> *I remember all the good times I spent sightseeing with my parents*
> > *I remember the life I spent with my heroic parents*
> > *working hard like a bee*
> *Treating me luxuriously for a great childhood*
> > *spoiling me and providing me with a happy childhood*
> *My childhood place, across the mountain*
> > *I remember it forever, always keeping it in my mind*
> *Irrespective of the life of suffering caused by our oppressors*
> > *I am thinking of you here in the trenches.*

The liberation front produced many songs and other works of art in musical and theatrical forms to capture the hearts and minds of the Eritrean population both at home and abroad. Songs such as "Message of Love to the Parents From Their Children in the Trenches" clearly showed the human side of the Eritrean armed struggle. The Kalashnikov was not Eritreans' weapon of choice. Young Eritrean men and women did not leave their families because of their love and passion for weapons. They left their loving families behind and chose to carry arms and live in the trenches because they had run out of all other options. They wanted freedom for their loved ones, the ones who would live to see the fruit of the tree that would grow on the remains of their bodies, the tree that would be fed their blood.

The brutality of both European and African colonizers made it difficult, if not impossible, for Eritreans to lead normal lives within their God-given territory. Eritreans tried genuinely appealing to the international community during the 1940s, but they were slapped with a federal union with Ethiopia. They tried fighting the federation through peaceful and nonviolent means during the 1950s, forming the Eritrean Liberation Movement, but the response was detention and arbitrary execution by the Ethiopian armed forces. Finally, Eritreans were left without any other option except to pick up the rifle and fight for their existence. The successive Ethiopian governments responded to Eritreans' uprising through mass killings and burning villages and towns. Ethiopians' brutality and inhumane treatment of Eritreans was supported through the flow of arms from Washington, Tel Aviv, Moscow, Havana, Tripoli, Aden, and Pyongyang, first in the name of preserving and defending the king of the "Christian island surrounded by an Islamic sea"[28] and then in the name of expanding Comintern in the Horn of Africa.

Our musical program was to end at two a.m., but the crowd would not let us stop. People kept dancing till four in the morning. In a single evening of September 1990, we were able to raise close to a quarter of a million Kenyan shillings (about $10,000 US) for the liberation front. We were hugely proud to send the cash collected from our concert, along with additional money made by selling videotapes of the show, to the field. We had done our part, and that made us feel a bit closer to home.

And yet, the following day, as on the previous days, we all had to go back to our reality of refugee life: aggressively working on our resettlement processes that were going to pave the way for us to go as far away from home as the foreign embassies would allow. Some of us were looking forward to resettling in the United States of America, some in Canada, some in Australia, and some in Europe. We were basically going to be scattered all over the world.

Our family resettlement process went much smoother than a lot of our compatriots'. Most of our compatriots languished in the slums of Eastleigh and the tents of Thika refugee camp for many years. Some of our friends stayed in Kenya for more than ten years waiting for resettlement. In no small part due to our oldest brother Afewerki's diligence

28   Quoted in *The Lion of Judah in the New World* by Theodore Vestal, originally from a memo from John Foster Dulles.

and commitment, and with a tremendous amount of help from Abraham Kahsay, a young Eritrean who grew up in Kenya, our resettlement process was completed in an expeditious manner. Afewerki sent us all the documents needed from our sponsor, the Fourth Presbyterian Church, and the International Office for Migration, the organization that coordinated the migration process. Abraham Kahsay helped us fill out the voluminous and sometimes overwhelming resettlement application forms required by the United States Embassy and the IOM. The completeness of the documentation minimized the number of appointments and how often we had to go back and forth with the US consulate in Nairobi.

Once we submitted the required application forms with our sponsorship documentation to the US Embassy in Nairobi, we were called for an interview within five months. Abraham Kahsay interpreted for us during the interview. After we passed the interview, it took another three to four months for medical examination and travel arrangements. All in all, we stayed in Kenya for a year and three months. Once our family resettlement process to the US was finalized, Lemlem and I boarded a Pan American World Airways flight around eleven p.m. on Thursday, November 29, 1990. We stopped over in London's Heathrow airport, and our flight resumed to New York's John F. Kennedy airport. After clearing immigration and customs at JFK, we boarded another flight to Washington, DC. Eden's process was delayed for three additional months because Afewerki had to travel to Kenya from the US in order to officially marry her before he could sponsor her as his wife.

NEW LIFE AND NEW DREAMS OF A HIGH SCHOOL DROPOUT

"I know how men in exile feed on dreams."
—Aeschylus

Lemlem and I landed at Dulles International Airport during the early afternoon of Saturday, December 1, 1990. Afewerki picked us up and drove us to his apartment in Silver Spring, Maryland. Jet-lagged and exhausted, we slept until late into the next morning.

During breakfast Lemlem and I began asking Afewerki what we needed to start school. Afewerki suggested that we relax for a while and enjoy the Christmas holiday season. He said he would get us registered for school in time to start the spring semester, which would begin at the end of January or in early February.

I protested, saying, "Afewerki, I think we have squandered enough time. We need to get back to school as soon as possible!"

Afewerki tried to reason with us. "You've been through a lot! Can't you take a day or two to catch your breath? After all, there is a process you have to go through in order to register for school in America, and the second semester doesn't start till February anyway."

From the tone of his voice, Lemlem and I could sense the image Afewerki had of us. It was clear he still thought of us as his baby siblings who would need his active assistance and guidance. He was planning to show us around and help us navigate Washington, Baltimore, and the rest of the metro area. Afewerki loves America, and he wanted us to see the great nation for what it was. He wanted to show us how things worked in America so that we would love the country the way he did. He even rented an apartment with two bedrooms in the White Oak area of Silver Spring, Maryland, an affluent neighborhood in Montgomery County. By making this choice, he was stretching himself financially so that he could send his baby sister and brother to some of the finest public schools in the area. He had a wonderful plan for his siblings.

The only problem was that this plan did not take into account all that Lemlem and I had gone through to get to America. He didn't realize we were not the same babies we were when he left home, and it never crossed his mind that we might have overgrown our natural ages.

To his credit, Afewerki himself had assumed responsibilities that could easily have overwhelmed others. Unlike many at his age, Afewerki had become a parent of his two siblings, not an easy task for someone who had migrated to the United States only about three years earlier.

Afewerki had big plans for us, but those plans were diametrically opposed to the plans we had in mind for ourselves. He did not know that we had no intention of staying in the US any longer than needed. All we wanted was to get our schooling done and go back home to the independent Eritrea we had been dreaming of for a while. Education, we felt, was the only thing standing between us and our dream of going back home. We were sure about it.

What Lemlem and I did not realize—but would soon find out—was that we had an inaccurate perception of ourselves. Thanks to the political education that instilled a strong sense of identity, coupled with the independent living in Kenya, our egos were inflated beyond reason. We thought we knew it all and that things must be done our way!

We went back and forth on the topic of school registration, and finally we made it clear to Afewerki that there was no way we would stay home for even two weeks, let alone two months. When our discussions got heated, Afewerki woke up. He took control of the situation. He promised to call his job and request the next day off so he could take us to the Board of Education and see what we needed to start the registration process. Afewerki tried to hide his feelings, but his frustration was clearly visible.

Afewerki took Lemlem and me to the offices of the Montgomery County Public Schools in Rockville, Maryland, and explained our situation to an official. There, we learned that we would need to make an appointment to take English and math assessment exams. The administrator gave Afewerki some booklets that explained the exams and contained sample questions. We left with a study guide to prepare ourselves.

At the mention of a placement exam, my eagerness and confidence started to decline. We thought we would automatically be enrolled at the high school level because we were already in high school in Eritrea. We really didn't think we could pass a high school English exam. But after reviewing the booklet, we felt a lot better, and we went back to the Board of Education just two days later. I got a passing score in both math and English and found out that my command of written English and grammar was much better than my ability to speak the language. I did well in the reading and grammar parts of the test, but lost points in the writing section. I'd never had any training in writing, and I did my best to cover half a page in the writing exercise.

The books I had read as a child in Eritrea and Kenya seemed to have paid off.

Based on our results, I was placed at Springbrook High School in Silver Spring. Since Lemlem needed more assistance with her language skills, she was assigned to Albert Einstein High School, one of the Montgomery County high schools that offered an English for Speakers of Other Languages (ESOL) program. Finally, we had only to take medical exams and produce our immunization records before we could begin.

On Sunday, a week after our arrival, Afewerki took us to worship at the Ambassadors of Fourth Presbyterian Church, the church that sponsored our immigration to the US. Here we met our sponsors, including Dr. John Dalton, Dave Rysak,

Biff LeVee, and his mom, Luella Nash LeVee, who had become fast friends with Afewerki and had been largely responsible for our successful petition to come to America.

We were welcomed by Dave Rysak and Dr. John Dalton and the rest of the congregation. They surrounded us, asking questions about Eritrea and how we were finding America. Everyone we encountered was warm and friendly. They all had Bibles in their hands. When the service began, the pastor leading the congregation announced our arrival with great enthusiasm and pointed us out. All eyes turned back in our direction. This was a new and unique experience.

When the service ended, Dave Rysak came back with us to our apartment, and Lemlem and I started getting to know him better.

Dave told us that he was born Francis Dave Rysak in December of 1958 to parents of Polish, Russian, and German descent. Dave grew up living with his grandparents on his mother's side, along with his parents and his sister, Dolly. There were six of them in the house his grandfather bought in 1923 in Tarentum, Pennsylvania. Dave accepted Jesus Christ as his lord and savior when he was thirteen years old. He went to Oral Roberts University in Tulsa, Oklahoma, where he studied telecommunications and business administration. Dave worked his way through college, although he received a full scholarship that covered his expenses during the last two years. After graduating from ORU, Dave worked for the NBC TV affiliate in Tulsa for a year and a half, then quit and went back to school to start work on his MBA degree.

Graduate school lasted only one summer before Dave dropped out and started freelancing in the TV industry. He did everything—ushering concerts, parking cars, operating a spotlight for shows and operas, unloading trucks for concerts, rigging lights, working the gaffe ring for film shoots, operating a slow motion camera for college sporting events, and later traveling across the county shooting sales presentations for corporations. Dave called this period in his life "creative unemployment."

He originally went to Washington, DC, for a freelance job at WTTG TV-5 that lasted three months. Liking the area, he moved everything to DC while he looked for a full-time job. He lived in a garage until he got an apartment in the Bethesda area. After three months, Dave took the full-time job at the TV station where he would end up working for many years.

Dave searched out many churches in the area and ended up at the Ambassadors of Fourth Presbyterian Church in Bethesda, Maryland. He got involved in the church's singles group in the mid-1980s. It was there that he met Afewerki, whom the ambassadors had sponsored to come to America. Afewerki was part of Dave's small discussion group on Sunday mornings. Dave and Afewerki later became fast friends at an ambassadors' retreat in West Virginia. From that time on they spent a lot of time together outside of church. For a while they lived only a block apart and shared meals almost every night.

Ambassadors of Fourth Presbyterian Church was sponsoring a mission trip to Kenya in the summer of 1990. Dave went with a group of seven to Nairobi, Mombasa, and Narok, Kenya. Dave and I met at the time of his arrival in the Nairobi airport and later while he stayed in the city. After we came to America, we all spent time together. Eating each other's cooking always seemed to be part of our visits.

All in all, it took us two weeks to get registered for school.

Afewerki took me to Springbrook High on my first day, and we were led to the counselor's office. My counselor was named Beatrice Newel; she would be my guiding light for my entire tenure at Springbrook and beyond. Afewerki gave Bea my completed paperwork, and she explained to us how things worked at the school and the dates for the coming semester. When Bea saw Afewerki translating for me, she spoke to me directly.

"Hi," she said.

"Hi!" I responded, greeting her with whatever broken English I could muster. I also asked Bea if I could start school immediately, without waiting for the next semester.

She turned to Afewerki and told him that I spoke good enough English and that, seeing my test results, she did not think I needed help with translation. I didn't know what she was thinking; I wasn't at all confident about my English. At any rate, Bea told Afewerki that he did not have to come to school with me again and I would do fine on my own. She also said I could start school in the current semester, but I would not be able to get credit for the classes. That made my day. Who cared about credit? All I wanted was to sit in a classroom and learn. Bea assigned a student to show me around, and I was astonished to learn that I would be going from room to room for my classes. I was used to having all my classes in one room, with the teachers coming and going. Initially, I did not think I would be able to find my way around Springbrook High School. I thought the school was huge and the rooms were too similar to separate one from another.

On Monday, December 17, 1990, one week before Christmas break, I started school in America.

On my second week at Springbrook, I was sitting alone in the library. A tall young African American student came into the library and sat across from me. He said, "I am Jevo. What is your name?"

That one was easy. I said, "Dawit," and he started talking. He spoke very fast, and although I didn't understand, I kept nodding and saying "yes" and "okay." Finally, when the bell rang, we both got up and left the library.

The next day around the same time I went to the same spot, where I had been sitting for the past few days. Jevo came again and said, "What's up?"

I had no clue what that meant and responded by saying, "What do you mean?"

He repeated, "You know, what's up, like, hi."

So I asked him how I was supposed to respond. He told me I could say, "Fine," and I repeated it: "Fine." Then he launched into another burst of fast talking that I couldn't catch, but he seemed a bit upset this time.

I decided to come clean and asked him to speak slowly. Finally, I understood that he was asking me why I had not come to the game the day before. "What game?" I asked. He looked astonished. Finally seeming to understand my situation, he told me—speaking slowly this time—that the day before he had asked me to join the soccer team and invited me to a practice that afternoon. Apparently, with all my nodding, I had given him the impression that I had accepted his invitation, and he'd been expecting me to show up for the soccer practice. Jevo was from Cameroon, and when he saw me with my Afro, sitting alone, he rightly deduced that I was from Africa and, thus, I played soccer well. This was the kind of misunderstanding that plagued my communications with peers in the early days at Springbrook. I thanked Jevo for the invitation and told him that I wouldn't be able to stay after school to play soccer. I had no time, considering the insurmountable amount of work I had to do in order to catch up at school.

During the next semester, though, something interesting happened in my PE class. While we were playing indoor soccer, one of my classmates approached me and said, "Hey, is your name like David or something? Can we call you David when we want you to pass the ball? We can't remember your name."

I looked at my teammate with a blank face. I was not sure how to respond to what I perceived to be an absurdity. I finally said, "Yes, you are right, Dawit means David in English. But that is not my name. My name is Dawit and I only respond to that name. You have two options: either you call me Dawit or you don't get the ball." It didn't take them long to start calling me Dawit, and soon I could happily pass the ball as I saw fit.

"Dawit" and "Eritrea" are two words I made sure people knew how to say and spell.

During the last three weeks of the fall semester, one of the classes I attended was lab science. At the end of the semester, the teacher asked the class if we were ready with our presentations. Almost all the students roared with excitement. They all said in unison they were ready. The teacher started calling names, and each student in turn stood up to present their scientific skills. I observed each presentation closely and noticed that some were showing some tricks using white papers and some were showcasing their skills with cards. Finally, my turn arrived. I asked the student sitting in the front row to give me the deck of cards he had used to showcase his scientific skill set. He passed the deck to me, and I walked toward the front of the class. None of them had any way of knowing what I could do with cards, but I had played cards and performed tricks with cards since second grade.

When I reached the blackboard, I turned around and faced the class. I told them I was going to show them a trick whereby I would be able to know the face of a card that was facing them. I put both my hands behind my back. Then I brought the deck of cards forward and asked the class to call out the face of the card. "Jack of spades," they shouted with one loud voice. I smiled and put my arms behind me for the second time, brought the deck of cards forward again, and then I was the one to tell them the face of the second card. I repeated the process a few times before they were convinced that I could magically tell the faces of all the cards without looking. They were impressed and kept asking me how I did it.

The trick to this game was simply to show the front of the deck of cards to the students while having the last card facing me. Each time I put my hands behind my back, I was bringing the card that was facing me to the front of the deck while flipping the next to last card to face me so that on the next round I could then bring that one to the front. Thus, the card that was facing me would face outward on each successive round, and I could call it because I had seen it on the prior round. The teacher was impressed enough to give me an A for the science lab exam.

Eden joined us after three months. Here in the United States, same as in Addis Ababa and Nairobi, Eden and Lemlem became my surrogate mothers. Since the day I left home, both Eden and Lemlem made sure that I did not have to lift a finger at home. The only thing I blame my two sisters for is that they became impediments to developing my cooking skills. These two made sure that I never had to worry about the next meal.

A few weeks after Eden's arrival, a young lady named Judith Dean and her friend from Ambassadors of Fourth Presbyterian Church started coming to our apartment to tutor Lemlem and Eden. Thanks to Judy and her friend, both Eden and Lemlem started to improve their understanding and use of the English language significantly. Lemlem also started to excel academically.[29]

29 At the moment, Dr. Judith M. Dean is a professor of international economics with specializations in international economics, economic development, and econometrics at Brandeis University in Boston, Massachusetts.

Life at Springbrook High School was never dull. During the spring of 1991, I came to school wearing a designer sweater. I had a shirt that matched one of the colors in the sweater. The sweater was warm and colorful. As usual, I went to my art class, sat at my desk, and started working on my project. One of the students looked at me and said, "Hey, who gave you that sweater?" I looked at him in shock. I started to sweat. For a reason I could not pinpoint, I felt ashamed. How did he know somebody else gave me the sweater? Was there some identifying mark on the sweater that I did not see?

I finally decided to lie and replied, "I bought it from a shop in Silver Spring."

This guy rudely said, "I didn't ask where you got it from. I asked who gave it to you."

Was I furious! But I decided to stick with my story and told him I bought it from a shop near the Metro station in Silver Spring. He went back to his work and I went back to mine.

Unfortunately, I was so shocked and upset by the random-seeming attack that I barely got anything done in art class that day. Right after the bell rang, I ran to the restroom. I took off the sweater and examined it closely, looking for anything that would indicate Dave Rysak had given it to me. I turned it inside out, examining every inch of it. I saw nothing. Then I realized that the guy was trying to make a point: there was no way I could afford a sweater like that, and somebody must have given it to me. Well, the bitter truth was that he was right, and his insult hurt me badly—at least at the time.

In the same art class, on a different day, a girl came to my desk and started up a conversation—which consisted mostly of her asking me questions. Before she approached, I had noticed her and her friends talking and laughing while glancing toward me. When she came over and said hi, I felt a bit uneasy, wondering what she wanted and thinking what to say to her (and what not to say).

"Can I ask you a question?" she said.

When I nodded, she asked if I had seen a naked girl before, because she'd heard that in Africa we all walked around naked.

I stood frozen for a fraction of a second, and then decided to tell her the whole naked truth. "Yes, I have," I said. "You know, in Africa we all walk around naked. The men and women use leaves to cover their sexual organs. A lot of times, those leaves fall off when we jump from one tree to another. Then we all are naked."

She looked at me with wide-eyed wonder, and said, "Wow, so you've actually seen a naked girl?"

"Many times," I said, nodding sagely.

She went back to her cluster of friends, and they all started to laugh while glancing at me.

Every time I tell this story to one of my American friends (most of whom are either teachers or parents), they tell me that I was wrong to handle the situation the way I did, that all I did was make the students' ignorance worse. My take on it is that, at the time, my primary objective was to give those kids what they wanted to hear so they would get off my back. In fact, it was entertaining to me. I used to smile every time I saw those girls. In a way, it was a very successful defense mechanism: I had turned the joke on them, deflecting it away from myself. Their ignorance became the joke, as opposed to my supposed backwardness.

At home, when I saw the assignments Lemlem was working on, I really was disappointed by the rudimentary nature of what she was expected to know. I started to worry about what would happen if she continued to learn nothing year after year. I shared my worries with Bea and asked her to help us transfer Lemlem to Springbrook, which we accomplished the following semester.

When I look back at it now, the English for Speakers of Other Languages program seemed to me somewhat like trying to teach kids how to swim by letting them float comfortably on the surface using life jackets, never allowing them to hold their own against the water.

I took quite the opposite approach with my own life. I was taking regular English classes at Springbrook, and once I learned my way around the neighborhood, I started looking for a part-time job in the White Oak neighborhood. I searched for almost three months in vain.

Finally, Afewerki spoke to Alan Zins, one of his best friends. Alan talked to the management at K/B Congressional movie theaters in Rockville, and I applied there. Thanks to Alan Zins, I found my first job in America, earning $4.25 per hour.

Distance was one of the challenges with working at K/B Congressional movie theaters. Depending on the time of the day, I had to take two buses to go from White Oak to Congressional Plaza, where the movie theater was located. The biggest challenge was when I had to work the late-night shifts on Fridays and Saturdays. There were times when I had to close at three on Saturday morning and show up at ten a.m.

on the same day to open for the matinee. We addressed this challenge as a family by having Afewerki, after leaving work, drive his car to Rockville, leave his car at the Congressional Plaza, then take the bus back to White Oak. I would drive Afewerki's car back to White Oak during the wee hours.

My academic plan was simple: I was determined to graduate from high school in four years, attend two years of community college, and then transfer to a four-year university. If everything worked out well, I would have my bachelor's degree in ten years—four years in high school, two years in community college, and four years in a university. Then I would return home. I asked Bea, my counselor, what I needed in order to execute this plan. She gave me the exact information I was looking for: I would need twenty-three credit hours and passing grades on the Maryland state exams in math; national, state, and local government; and written and verbal English.

In the middle of all this, before I even finished one semester in an American high school, my home country got its independence. On May 24, 1991, Eritreans finally won their independence against all odds, having fought for liberation against the Italians, the British, and the Ethiopian governments in succession. Unlike any other African nation, Eritreans had to fight both white European colonizers and a black African colonizer that was uniquely supported and armed to the teeth by the two superpowers of the Cold War era, the United States of America and the Union of Soviet Socialist Republics.

The Eritrean People's Liberation Front liberated Eritrea one village, one town, and one city at a time, finally marching to the capital city of Asmara. The freedom fighters built strong civic institutions and public services including schools, health centers, a judiciary, and social services as they liberated each village and town. The balance of power eventually shifted in favor of the freedom fighters in March 1988, when the EPLF overtook the town of Afabet, capturing ten thousand Ethiopian soldiers and three senior Russian military advisers. Unheard of in the history of guerrilla warfare, the Eritrean freedom fighters released the ten thousand Ethiopian prisoners of war and the three Russians to the Red Cross.

The freedom fighters paraded into Asmara with their tanks and armored vehicles from the four checkpoints set up by the Ethiopian government. The residents of Asmara gave the freedom fighters the duly deserved hero's welcome. Mothers ululated at the sight of their children storming from the four entries to the cities. Many young men and women welcomed their heroes by rushing and jumping on top of the tanks and the armored vehicles. The rest were embracing and hugging the freedom fighters who were entering the city on foot and running alongside their heroes. For over twenty years, the four entries to the city had been heavily fortified by Ethiopian soldiers strip-searching every Eritrean entering or leaving Asmara. Now, the same gates were overtaken by the incoming freedom fighters and the people who had been eagerly waiting their arrival for decades. The euphoria and celebration across Asmara—across Eritrea—continued for the rest of the weekend and throughout the following week. The struggle was definitely long and bitter, but victory was certain indeed.

For something as precious and as priceless as freedom and independence, someone has to believe in it in order to see it. Eritreans wholeheartedly believed in the possibility of their independence since that fateful Sunday, November 12, 1899, when they broke out of Nakura prison. It had been ninety-one years, seven months, and a week, or 33,457 days, since Eritreans lit the torch of a united resistance against successive colonizers. Had those Eritrean legends not broken out of Nakura prison on that fateful Sunday, future generations would have known "only the names of those who have made Italy great" or, for that matter, only those who had made Ethiopia great. Eritreans now know the names of those who made Eritrea great.[30]

Eritreans' struggle for liberty and independence went through many ups and downs depending on the nature and alliance of each colonizer, but the defiance and resistance against oppression and subjugation never ceased to exist in various forms.

Eritreans finally attained their independence on Friday, May 24, 1991.

30 Woldeyesus, Winta. "Settlement of Societies in Eritrea." *Eritrea—Ministry of Information,* 2009. http://www.shabait.com/about-eritrea/history-a-culture/212-settlement-of-societies-in-eritrea.

RENEWED AMBITIONS AT SPRINGBROOK HIGH SCHOOL

"I know what hard work's about. I still come back
to what my strategy always was and will continue
to be: I'm not the smartest guy, but I can outwork
you. It's the one thing that I can control."
—Mayor Michael Bloomberg, *New York Magazine*

At the time Eritrea gained its independence, I was finishing my first semester at Springbrook High. I cannot say I was caught by surprise, considering Massawa, the largest port in the country, had been liberated eighteen months earlier. Yet I had a dilemma in that I was not prepared to go home. I chose to postpone my return home. I considered it would take me at least four years to finish high school, two years of prep courses to earn an associate degree at Montgomery College, and another two to complete my bachelor's degree at the University of Maryland. If all went well, I would be able to go back home for good by 1999.

By this time, Afewerki was contemplating moving us out of the apartment in White Oak. The rent was just too much for my brother and his wife, Eden, the only two breadwinners, to bear. Lemlem and I were not able to contribute much financially. I was making only $4.25 an hour and, because of school, could not work more than twenty-five or thirty hours per week. I could barely sustain my school expenses with that income, let alone contribute to the family's budget. At any rate, Afewerki was quickly able to find a two-bedroom apartment in another part of Silver Spring for almost half of what we were paying at White Oak, and we moved there during the summer of 1991.

Our new neighborhood was heavily populated by Hispanics and recent immigrants from Africa and Asia. The apartment was located right on the border of Montgomery County, one of the most affluent counties in the region, and Prince George's County, one of the least affluent. I am sure Afewerki took into account when he chose our new home that the apartment was located just within the borders of the Montgomery County school district. Lemlem and I remained at Springbrook and did not have to face the challenges of adjusting to a new school.

With Bea's recommendation, I decided to take one social studies class during the summer of 1991. We figured it would be best for me to take the NSL government and contemporary issues class during the summer and take the Maryland state–required NSL government exam as well. Thanks to Bea, it was perfect timing for me; I could take the state-required exam right after taking the class. That I did. I had one of the three requirements for graduation out of the way.

I had enjoyed using the Apple computer for my English writing assignments during my first semester at Springbrook; I decided to register for a computer programming class in the fall semester of the 1991–92 school year. The computer programming language taught at Springbrook at the time was Pascal. During the first week of class, Jim Haber, our teacher, started to familiarize us with the function keys (F1 through F12). Mr. Haber told the class to press F5. I did. Nothing appeared to change on my screen. I pressed the letter F and the number five again and again. But still nothing changed. The monitor of the computer still displayed the same screen. I glanced to my left and right sides, and the screens on both sides appeared to have changed. Mr. Haber said to press F1. I pressed the letter F and the number one. Nothing changed on my screen. Yet the screens on my left and right side changed. I did not want to interrupt the teacher, because I did not want to feel stupid. I believed everybody else was getting it right except me. I also was afraid that if Mr. Haber knew I was having that much difficulty the first week, he might kick me out of the class. So I decided to just make sure I looked busy till the class ended. I would ask one of the other students after school. I stayed after class, and thanks to my classmates I was able to recognize the function keys at the top of the keyboard and their intended purpose.

After a few weeks of lectures and class work, we were given a programming project where the grade was based on three aspects of the program we were assigned to write:

program execution, compilation, and style. Does the software program we wrote run successfully (execute the written instructions and give the user the intended output)? Does the program compile successfully (is the syntax of the entire program written correctly)? Are the procedures and functions (subroutines) of the program readable and properly documented?

Unfortunately, the program I wrote did not run properly—it just kept terminating with an error. It also did not compile. The compiler exited with numerous syntax errors.

For style, we had to adhere to Mr. Haber's "hand rule." Mr. Haber would lay down the printout of our computer programs. He then would stretch his thumb and little finger as far apart from each other as he could. If Mr. Haber was not able to touch with his fingers the beginning and the end of each subroutine (function or procedure), then he would take a point for each function that failed the hand rule. Proper documentation of the program was the second part of the grade for style. My program failed both Mr. Haber's hand rule and documentation. As such, the grades I obtained for my first Pascal project were F for execution, F for compilation, and F for style (it was undocumented "spaghetti" code).

At first, I thought there must be something wrong with me. I convinced myself something must change. Early in the morning, I was handed a note from my homeroom teacher, saying my counselor wanted to see me during lunch. When I appeared, Bea asked about my classes, and I told her all was fine. She said, "What about Pascal?" and I knew I was in trouble. I told Bea that it was not easy, but I was learning a lot in the class.[31]

Bea changed the subject and told me that Lemlem and I might be able to graduate earlier. We might not have to spend the entire four years in high school. I was not sure what she meant, considering we had just been talking about my shortcomings in the computer programming class.

It turned out Bea had been able to get both Lemlem and me six credits, one year's worth, for classes we had completed in Eritrea. When we first registered at Springbrook, I told Bea that I had finished my freshman year and Lemlem had attended two years of high school in Asmara. But since we did not have official transcripts or any other documentation of this fact, Bea had told us it wouldn't be possible to get credit for those classes. To my surprise, however, it seemed Bea had believed our claims and found a way to get us most of those credits.

In the end, Lemlem and I were each given credit for one year's worth of foreign languages, world history, social studies, algebra, science, and vocational education. To this day I have no idea how Bea managed to do it, but it saved us a lot of time.

Additionally, I was given credit for the three weeks I attended during the first semester of the 1990–91 school year by using the results I earned on the final exams as my semester grades. I managed to get one year of social studies out of the way by taking NSL government and contemporary issues

31 Years later I learned from Bea that Mr. Haber had apparently informed her that I was having difficulties in the class and it was likely that I might not be able to make it through the semester. I would not have disagreed with Mr. Haber's assessment if I were in his position.

during the summer. Thus, based on Bea's assessment of the number of credit hours I had acquired so far, it appeared that I could go straight into my junior year! All I had to do was find a way to get three more years of English classes out of the way and, of course, pass the required Maryland reading and writing exams.

That meant that—all of a sudden—it was time for me (actually, for Bea) to start considering colleges. It is amazing the kind of miracle a well-rounded, dedicated, and compassionate counselor can bring to a student's life. Who was this miracle maker? Beatrice Newel!

Beatrice Newel was born on November 15, 1952, in West Berlin, Germany, to Ruth Clara and Heinz Paul Hermansa. Bea's parents had met a year earlier in a dance club. Her father had just returned from Hanover, where, after being released from a prison camp, he worked as an interpreter for the British occupying forces. Her mother, who had studied fashion design in Dresden, East Germany, had fled to West Berlin to avoid conscription in a Russian work camp. Both of Bea's parents were unemployed when she was born. They lived in a sublet room on the Residenzstrasse in Reinickendorf, a northern borough of Berlin which was then under French occupation. Her mother found work doing alterations for a dry cleaning business next to the flat where they lived and was occasionally lucky enough to have clients who could commission new dresses and coats. Bea spent the first six years of her life in the constant company of her mother, often playing near the old Singer sewing machine.

She learned by age three how to knit, crochet, embroider, and sew. Bea's father tried to make a living as vacuum cleaner salesman but was not successful. But since he spoke English and Spanish fluently, he ultimately secured employment with the American troops. He worked his way up from a translator/interpreter to become the director of finance and budget for the US Army in Berlin. He worked for the army until he retired in 1989.

Bea's early childhood was influenced by living in a bombed-out and destroyed city. Wherever the family went, there were burned-out buildings, rubble, and debris. The streets looked like a mouth full of decaying teeth with an occasional tooth—i.e., house—intact.

Bea went to the Ruebezahlschule for elementary school. She was a sickly child, suffering illnesses that continued throughout her first few years of schooling—learning this I was reminded of my own childhood illness that almost killed me. In spite of her afflictions, Bea was at the top of her class and pretty much remained among the top three students during her entire primary and secondary education.

Bea started to study English in fourth grade. Her father was an active supporter of her schooling, quizzing her nightly on her English vocabulary and reviewing her math and science work. Her mother, on the other hand, would review Bea's Deutschklasse—German instruction—and help Bea with geography and history.

Germany began to prosper in the late 1950s, and the family was able to move into a larger apartment with a street view. She began high school at the Bertha von Suttner Gymnasium in Reinickendorf. The school specialized in modern languages.

When Bea began, the school had roughly ninety students. By exam time the group had shrunk to thirty-six students, the others forced to repeat classes or dismissed from the school.

The rigor of the curriculum at the Bertha von Suttner Gymnasium in Reinickendorf required that studying be the defining theme of Bea's high school years. After school, where she went six days a week, Bea would come home, have a snack, and work until ten or eleven p.m. This daily routine was interrupted only by the supper hour, when the family ate together.

Bea shared the top spot in her graduating class with her best friend, Barbara. Upon graduation Bea left for the United States and attended Blue Ridge Community College in Staunton, Virginia; Montgomery County Community College in Rockville, Maryland; and James Madison University in Harrisonburg, Virginia, earning a BA in German and French literature and language with a minor in education (summa cum laude and with distinction in German) and an MEd in counseling psychology (summa cum laude).

I've often felt that Bea was such a good counselor for me because she knew firsthand the difficulties of war and the challenges of immigrant life. I heard my story in hers, and I too was motivated to succeed as she had.

I have heard some motivational speakers define luck as "preparation plus opportunity." But I honestly can't say that I was prepared for the opportunity that came my way next; I believe it was sheer luck.

During the second semester of the 1991–92 school year at Springbrook, the soft-spoken and extremely patient honors physics teacher, Mr. Henderson, put the word out that he was looking for someone to attend a physics conference at Johns Hopkins University. Two students were selected, but a couple of days before the conference one of them dropped out for personal reasons. My seat in the class happened to be next to hers, and when Mr. Henderson looked in my direction I nodded, accepting the offer without knowing anything about the conference. It was to be on a Saturday and that was not a good day for me, as weekends were the only time I could put in more hours at the movie theater. But I was more interested in visiting a college campus than in my part-time, low-wage job.

I attended the physics conference and enjoyed it, although most of the material was way over my head. The best part of my visit was that I fell in love with the city of Baltimore and the Homewood campus.

The idea of attending Hopkins came into my head. However, I knew right away I did not belong there. I was a realist and knew the improbability of my making it back to the Hopkins campus again. It was, nevertheless, an experience I could not forget. And for whatever it was worth, when the conference ended I filled in my name and my address on a small card that was handed out to attendees and turned it in.

During the second semester of that same school year, Bea took me to the career and college counseling office at Springbrook and introduced me to Carolyn Finegar, whose job was to help students with their decisions about life after high school. Would they go to a four-year college or a different kind of school? Would they go directly to work? Were they ready for whatever direction their lives would take?

I told Carolyn about myself. She asked about my classes and how I was doing in them. I told her I had some A's and some B's. After she'd spent a few minutes viewing my records on the computer, Carolyn showed me a list of scholarships and started guiding me through the application process. I decided to apply for the Project Excellence scholarship, and she and I started working together on my essay.

Carolyn would frequently ask me, "Have you done anything for fun lately?"

My usual answer was, "Don't worry, I am having a lot of fun going to school here." Sometimes I would tell her about the parties and gatherings I attended at the Eritrean Community and Civic Center on Sixth and L Streets in northwest Washington. The center was my sanctuary and home away from home. While I certainly enjoyed these times, what Carolyn did not know was that I had not come to the United States to have fun. The kind of fun my classmates engaged in seemed to me to be a luxury I could not afford. Education was my goal, and I pursued it with near total focus.

Carolyn came to Springbrook after many years of raising her own children and being heavily involved in volunteer work. She was born in 1942 in the small town of Logan, West Virginia. In 1946, her family moved to Huntington, West Virginia. She grew up loving Huntington but not learning much about people from other cultures. She went to college locally, graduating from Marshall University with majors in English and biological science.

She left West Virginia after college and moved to Silver Spring. She married Wayne Finegar and had two children, a son and a daughter.

The move to Maryland opened up Carolyn's life in a myriad of exciting ways. She soaked up experiences and impressions from the many people she met in this rich, multicultural environment.

As her own children grew and brought their friends to meet her, Carolyn discovered that her native curiosity and empathy gave her the ability to listen to young people in an open and nonjudgmental way. She discovered a perfect fit for these abilities as a career counselor in public high schools, where she spent many years until she retired.

Professional career and college counseling required an enormous amount of information and experience, and she was just beginning to feel confident about her ability to help students when I walked into her life.

During my senior year, there were to be yet more important, influential adults in my life. Elizabeth Offutt, my advanced placement calculus teacher, was one of them. Ms. Offutt suggested that I join the Mu Alpha Theta Math Club, which promoted the appreciation of mathematics. At first I hesitated, weighing the amount of time I would have to commit after school, but I jumped in when Ms. Offutt told me that membership in the club would help me with my college applications. Mu Alpha Theta Math Club allowed me to visit a number of Montgomery County high schools for the various competitions, and I also got to know Ms. Offutt well during practice for the competitions.

One day, when we were talking about life in our respective countries, she said, "Dawit, I am sure you will go back home one day, but not to live. I was once certain beyond any doubt that I would return to Hungary. But once I visited home and stayed for two months, I realized how much things at home had changed. I also realized how much I had changed. You will see once you get a chance to visit your homeland."

I was not sure what she meant by that. I shrugged off the idea that I would never be able to live in Eritrea again.

Around this time, some of my classmates started asking what my rank was. I did not know what they meant—I just knew I would graduate in the spring. Finally, during lunch one day someone explained to me that all seniors were ranked based on grade point average. I smiled and turned back to my food.

I stared at the food in front of me and felt tears come to my eyes. I was not sad. I just remembered something from a few years back—back to the years when fierce competition at school was almost everything we lived for. I thought back to the eighth grade, when my best friend Daniel Mebrahtu tracked the grades of every student he thought had a chance of placing in the top three in the grade. He had a notebook where he kept the grades of each potential challenger for a unit rank. After every exam, Dani would ask for our grades. If we refused to divulge them, he would ask other people, and before the end of the week he would have each of our grades for each subject with the running totals computed. The tears were because I realized how much I missed Dani and my boyhood classmates. I missed the active and passionate competition. I missed it all.

I woke up from the daydream when the bell rang, walked to the trash can and threw away my lunch without having eaten a single bite. But I walked to my next class with a smile on my face, suddenly happier for having communed with my old friends, if only through sheer memory.

In order to fulfill the four years of English requirements for graduation, I took both English 11 and English 12 during my senior year. The first semester of English 11 class with Debra Adkins covered medieval arts. Mrs. Adkins assigned each student to work on a research project. I was assigned maize. Based on the number of summer vacations and holidays I spent in Adi-Hayo, my ancestral village, I didn't think I was going to have a problem planting maize seed—corn—in a vase full of dirt.

A couple of weeks later, some students brought part of their work to class to show to Mrs. Adkins. Mrs. Adkins asked me how my project was coming, and I told her it was coming along well and she would really be impressed. She told me to bring my work the following week for evaluation. I really was proud of myself by what I was able to accomplish. I put fertilizers on the vase. I watered the maize twice a day. I really took good care of it. I was looking forward to some compliments from Mrs. Adkins.

I put the vase on the table. Mrs. Adkins looked at the maize and then back at me. She appeared to be confused. I was confused. I did not know why she was staring at me and back at the maize. Then she said, "What is this?" I told her it was maize. Then she realized what had transpired. She smiled. I smiled, not knowing what was funny. Then she said, "This is corn. What does corn have to do with medieval art?" She opened one of the books on her table and showed me a picture of a maze. I read the word, which actually was spelled "maze," not "maize." Then I realized what was funny.

Mrs. Adkins was one of the amazing educators who truly believed in rewarding their students' efforts. If her students were able to show that they were trying their best in their work, she would provide many opportunities to get the grades they deserved.

I am not going to say Mrs. Adkins was a nice teacher, because she does not like the term due to its historical connotation. As taught by Mrs. Adkins, in the old English, the word *nice* used to mean "stupid, foolish, and senseless." Mrs. Adkins was not a nice teacher; she was an awesome teacher.

Mrs. Adkins gave me an additional week to work on my project, and I was able to turn it in for full credit—a representation of a maze game on a board—a week late. She still gave me an A grade for the project.

Nancy Abeshouse's personality was different than Mrs. Adkins's. Mrs. Abeshouse was a bit reserved and a no-nonsense teacher. I was really struggling in English 12. The major challenge I was facing was the fact that I had to study the vocabularies for both English 11 and English 12 classes on a weekly basis.

The vocabulary—synonyms, antonyms, and sentences using each word—I had to study had doubled. When I asked for help, Mrs. Abeshouse openheartedly welcomed me into to her home for additional tutoring. With her help, I was able to survive my last year of English courses at Springbrook.

During the first semester of my senior year, I received an application and a catalog from Johns Hopkins University. After reading the total cost was thirty-two thousand dollars per year, I trashed the documents to avoid any distraction from my schoolwork. After all, I could not afford to gamble seventy dollars for an application fee to a school I had no hope of getting into based on my academic performance—and even if I were to get in, I was sure I could not afford the high tuition. I would have to work way more than twenty hours a week to earn that kind of money.

A month or two later, I received another package from the Hopkins admissions office, dated December 3, 1992. It contained a letter along with the application package. The letter stated that I could qualify for an application fee waiver and that I could also request "an extension beyond our January 1 deadline" if I needed it. Talk about a school that would not take no for an answer! I started to wonder where the school had obtained my information, and I remembered the physics conference and the card I'd filled out with my address.

JOHNS HOPKINS
U N I V E R S I T Y

Office of Admissions

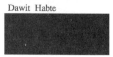

December 3, 1992

Dawit Habte

Dear Dawit,

Our January 1 application deadline is quickly approaching and I have been looking forward to receiving your application. As I was looking through our applications files, I noticed that we haven't received an application from you.

When I was applying to college, it seemed as if all of the deadlines occurred at the same time and the paper trail would not end. With all the things happening in your life right now, perhaps our application and deadline got buried in *"the pile."* Please find enclosed an additional application, just in case the original one you received was misplaced. Should you need an extension beyond our January 1 deadline, please let me know.

Don't forget that it is also possible to qualify for an application fee waiver. To see if you qualify, you need to check with your guidance counselor.

By this time, you have received a lot of information about Hopkins. However, you may have additional questions. If there is anything about Hopkins you don't know, please call me at ▮▮▮▮▮▮▮ I look forward to hearing from you.

Sincerely,

Jodi C. Hester

Jodi C. Hester
Assistant Director of Admissions

Enclosure

The most interesting and amazing part of this package was that it was sent to an address my family and I had left more than a year and a half earlier. It could easily have been returned to the sender and not been forwarded, especially since the old address was in my brother's name. Yet it found me at my new address. Since the letter said I could get a waiver for the application fee, I had nothing to lose by submitting an application. I decided to apply to Hopkins just for the heck of it.

I showed Bea and Carolyn the package. Bea started working on writing me a letter for the application fee waiver. Carolyn and I got to work on the application itself and my personal essay. I was determined to get it done before the official January 1 deadline, and to hand deliver the package to Baltimore if I had to. In the end, I mailed the package a week before the deadline.

On Saturday, March 20, 1992, I left my job at K/B movie theaters in Rockville around three p.m. and went to a scholarship interview with Project Excellence. During the presentation, one of the judges flipped through a couple of pages, looked at me, and asked me if I had gotten accepted to Brown University or Duke. I replied that I had not applied to those colleges, that I had only applied to Johns Hopkins, the University of Maryland, and Virginia Tech. He asked why I had checked off that I was seeking scholarships to attend Brown, Duke, and other universities if I hadn't applied to any of them. All I could do was stammer something to the effect of "I could not afford the application fees to those universities. I was planning to apply only if I get scholarship from Project Excellence."

Not long after that day, I received a letter of acceptance from Hopkins. They accepted 880 out of 8500 applicants.

On April 13, 1993, I received a surprising letter from Project Excellence with a partial scholarship to any university of my choice. That spring I graduated from Springbrook High School as a member of the National Honor Society, and in the fall I began my freshman year at Johns Hopkins University with a partial scholarship from Project Excellence and a partial scholarship from Hopkins.

My high school graduation. Left to right: my friend Haile Woldab, me, and my cousin Tecle Tesfamichael

LIFE AT JOHNS HOPKINS

"When you want something, all the universe
conspires in helping you to achieve it."
—Paulo Coelho, *The Alchemist*

In his book *His Excellency: George Washington*, Joseph J. Ellis wrote, "Because he lacked both the presumptive superiority of a British aristocrat and the economic resources of a Tidewater grandee, [George] Washington could only rely on the hard core of his own merit, his only real asset." When I arrived at Hopkins, the only real asset I possessed was time and a number of good people who wanted to see me succeed.

I went off to Hopkins with three goals in mind: to work hard on my education, to support myself financially by taking jobs on campus, and to find a way to bring my younger sister Akberet to the US to get medical treatment for hearing loss that started with an ear infection when she was a baby. Akberet had suffered a great deal as a result of this, and the doctor in Eritrea had finally told us our only option was to take her abroad and have her eardrum fixed surgically. I was now intent on making this happen.

To secure a job before school started, I went to the Homewood campus in July 1993 and applied for a student assistant position performing clerical work at the Office of Multicultural Students Affairs. In late August, a lady named Rose Varner-Gaskins called me in for an interview. I got the job and was told I could start as a work-study student when school opened for the fall semester.

During orientation week, I called Dr. Jack Dalton, one of the individuals who sponsored my siblings and me when we came to the US, and told him that I was at Hopkins. I could hear Jack's excitement at the news, and he asked when we could meet.

The next day he picked me up from campus and took me to CompUSA. I honestly had no idea why we were there; I just tagged along. But at the store he pointed to the desktop computers and told me to choose the one that I wanted. I picked a Gateway 486 DX PC with a CD-ROM. (At the time this was state of the art in the PC world.) Then we walked over to the printers. I selected an HP and a box of paper that would last me for years. I thought, *From this point on, I am armed with tools just as good as those of any other student on this campus.* It was time to prove that.

My second week on campus, I went to the Homewood Academic Computing lab to begin my computer programming assignment and noticed a flyer inviting students to apply for a proctoring position. The position was open to both work-study and non–work-study students. I applied right away for nights and weekends. As a proctor in the lab, I could play around with Unix, VMS, and VM operating systems. I also started familiarizing myself with Macintosh application packages and improving the narrow knowledge of DOS and Windows I had acquired in high school.

During Christmas break, I went back to Silver Spring to spend the weekend with my family. While we talked about life in Baltimore, one of our friends mentioned Professor Tekie Fessehatzion's name and gave me his number, saying he was a good person to reach out to for guidance. I was not sure what to do with the phone number, considering I had never heard of the professor. But I called him when I got back to campus the following week.

We met a week later at a coffee shop on the corner of St. Paul and Twenty-Ninth Streets and talked for a couple of hours. I actually did most of the talking, while he did most of the asking. We talked for five minutes about school and about our lives. Then the topic switched to Eritrea. As he later told me, Professor Tekie was very much impressed by how much I knew about Eritrea's history and its people.

Professor Tekie and I became two sides of a coin: I became a symbol of the young Eritrean student he always wished to teach, in need of tutelage and mentoring, and he became the mentor, guide, and father figure I dearly needed.

As a young man, Tekie was a bright student. One of his most vivid memories was the lowering of the Union Jack and hoisting of the Ethiopian flag in 1952 at the building where the Eritrean national assembly held their sessions. He was sitting across the street when officials from the Ethiopian government had taken it down and replaced it with the flag of Ethiopia.

Tekie left Eritrea for the United States in 1962, and in the following years he was awarded scholarships to attend some of the most prestigious universities in the United States of America.

Tekie earned his bachelor's degree in economics from the University of Connecticut, his master's degree from the State University of New York, and a doctorate in economics and social development from the University of Pittsburgh in 1976. He became a professor at various renowned American universities, including the University of Pittsburgh and Jackson State University in Mississippi. Professor Tekie was also a director of business and economic research at Jackson State University. Professor Tekie spent the last twenty years of his life as chair and professor of the department of economics at Morgan State University in Baltimore.

With respect to his intellectual excellence, Professor Tekie had become two things: an ardent advocate of African peasants and a loyal defender of his people and his country. Professor Tekie always considered the safety and protection of the poor, especially the African poor, as his primary point of reference. When dealing with economic development, he believed and advocated for the old proverbial physician's credo: first, do no harm. Here is what Professor Tekie wrote when discussing what he referred as the "Junkyard of Theories" that formed the basis for the formulation and implementation of development programs on the African continent: "Sometimes one wishes development theories were treated like new drugs—then they would be vigorously tested before they are tried on people to prevent possible harmful side effects."[32]

32 "Some Thoughts on the African Economic Predicament: Survival Strategies," 1985.

While he was undergoing radiation and chemo treatment for advanced brain cancer, Memhr Tekie repeatedly said, "The poor need to be supported." At first, I did not pay close attention to his words, but when he repeated the phrase, I basically asked him if he was trying to make amends with his God. Jokingly, I told him that he might be getting older, but not dying.

Apparently, Professor Tekie was neither an ideologue nor dogmatic, neither Marxist nor Jeffersonian. In fact Professor Tekie considered the elitists and the ideologues to be part and parcel of the predicaments ailing the African continent. Selflessly, Professor Tekie had identified "economists and other social scientists" as part of the predicament Africa faced. When explaining the predicament of the African continent, he wrote:

> "Since the late 1950s, Africa has attracted the attention of social scientists, mostly economists and political scientists, who in the course of their research on economic and political development advanced theories they claimed would explain the lack or slowness of economic growth in various African countries. While their theories have not done much to illuminate the sources of contemporary economic predicament or provide useful guidance for action, the proponents of these theories have been able to advance their career rapidly in American universities and the various aid offices."[33]

As an Eritrean nationalist, Professor Tekie believed in the sanctity of the nation:

33 Ibid.

"For people of my generation, Eritrea's independence is a dream come true. But as Ato Woldeab wrote in one of his essays in 1946, political independence is not sufficient. We should not rest until everyone, regardless of his or her station in life, is empowered to play a meaningful role in Eritrea's future. ... My plea to the young is to remain engaged in the life of our people. Whatever you do, do not, I repeat do not, take anything for granted. We are in a tough neighborhood. Our sovereignty will be tested again and again. Remain vigilant."[34]

For Professor Tekie to meet a young Eritrean who was born and raised during the Ethiopian colonization was like a breath of fresh air. In the minds of Eritreans of his age, there was a notion that my generation would be lost when it came to knowing and caring about Eritrea and its history.

I am not sure what I said to impress the professor, but from the day we met until his passing on April 19, 2010, Professor Tekie Fessehatzion was my mentor, confidant, and trusted friend.

As to my campus life, in the spring of 1994, I got a third job, as a teaching assistant in the computer science department for a course in Pascal—the programming language that had so confounded me at Springbrook. I was one of four Pascal TAs for that semester. My responsibilities included lecturing one hour a week, helping students during office hours (three hours per week), and grading programs, papers, and exams.

34 "Eritrean public intellectuals and the development of the national purpose."

Most of the students were juniors and seniors majoring in biochemical engineering, biophysics, physics, and electrical engineering, taking Pascal to fulfill their computer science requirements. There were a few sophomores and a couple of first-year students. Considering the majority of the students were upperclassmen, I felt sure there was nothing new I could teach them regarding following instructions and the need to turn in assignments on time.

At the Homewood Academic Computing lab, my manager promoted me from proctor to student consultant, with duties that included supporting various departments and groups on the campus. As a student consultant, some of my responsibilities were to answer questions in person and on the phone, teach departmental courses (beginner and advanced Unix and VAX/VMS operating systems), and prepare manuals and user handouts.

During this semester, too, I missed home terribly. But this time, instead of risking a sky-high phone bill that I would have to sell my books to pay off, I decided to make an audiotape and mail it to the family. I recorded both sides of a 180-minute tape and poured out all my grief to my mom. As I told her some of the fun things I was doing on campus, I cried bitterly at times and laughed at other times. Finally, I said my good-byes and mailed the tape the next day.

In December of 1994, when I went home for the first time in five years, my sister reminded me about that tape. She told me how much they had all enjoyed listening to it and that she had kept it in a safe place.

My first year at Hopkins ended with a mixed feeling: I could have done better academically, but I had a few decent on-campus jobs where I was earning money while learning practical skills. I was taking eighteen credit hours while working a total of sixty hours per week: twenty hours at the Office of Multicultural Student Affairs as a student assistant, twenty hours at Homewood Academic Computing as a student consultant, and twenty hours as a teaching assistant in the computer science department.

By the time I started my sophomore year, my cumulative GPA had dropped to B-minus. This was a major concern for me, especially since I was seriously considering going to medical school. It did not take me long to realize my areas of concern: I had overloaded myself. The solution was simple. Since I could not afford to lose any of my jobs, I had to cut down on my course load. For the fall semester of my sophomore year, in 1994, I registered for fifteen credit hours, the minimum requirement for full-time students.

The twenty hours I worked every weekend at Homewood Academic Computing was actually where I acquired most of my programming, computer support, and technical document writing skills. At the time, Homewood Academic Computing was the institution tasked with deploying and supporting new and cutting-edge technologies across the various schools and affiliates of Johns Hopkins University. Thanks to the generous donors and financiers of the university, we had unlimited and unfettered access to new and advanced technologies, both in hardware and software.

In the middle of the fall semester of my sophomore year, I was lying on my back, thinking of home, in the field known to students as the Beach across from the Eisenhower Library, on the Charles Street side of the Hopkins campus. I thought of friends and family. I thought of my sister Akberet and wondered how she was doing. I remembered when the doctor had told us the only hope for a permanent cure for Akberet's increasing hearing loss would be to go abroad and have her eardrum fixed surgically.

I started to think about what I could possibly do to help Akberet. I had asked Afewerki years before to find a way to bring her to the US. That did not go far for a number of reasons, including our struggle to get on solid footing ourselves. This time I could not ask my brother. He was married and it was time for him to start having his own kids. Besides, he had done his part by bringing Lemlem and me to the US. Thanks to Afewerki and Eden, we'd had a roof over our heads throughout our high school years. It was time that I stepped up to the challenge of the day. The burden felt heavy, but I still had to try.

Akberet's hearing problems had begun with an ear infection when she was just a baby. When I last saw her, about five years earlier, she was on the verge of losing her hearing altogether. We didn't know in the beginning what was going on. Mom would have to put cotton in her ears to stop the earwax from draining and running down her face; we would tease her, saying the reason she had so much earwax was because of her stubbornness. But one day my mom asked me to go with them to the doctor, and I was shaken to the core by what the doctor showed us. He pointed a lighted instrument—an otoscope—into my sister's ears and showed us the soft, bright red tissue inside. He informed us that her eardrums were completely destroyed, and worse, that there was nothing that could be done in Eritrea. We had visited this doctor on numerous occasions when Akberet's pain did not ease after cleaning the yellow substance that drained from her ears. This time the doctor told us there was no need to come back to him and waste our money; there was nothing he could do for her that we could not do at home. He told us to make sure to keep her ears dry and give her aspirin for the persistent headaches. We used to clean Akberet's ears by putting cotton at the end of a matchstick, as a substitute for Q-Tips. I had often wondered why Akberet could be so aggressive and short-tempered. I finally realized that the pain and discomfort from her chronic ear infections were making her irritable.

I needed money in order to sponsor Akberet to the US, and I did not have any. I thought of taking a couple of years off from school and working to make the money, but I got scared at the very notion of pausing my education. Mostly I worried about what people would say. I was afraid my Eritrean community would assume I got kicked out of Hopkins, a fine institution from which no sane person would willfully drop out. I was also scared of the idea of dropping out, not because I valued a Hopkins education more than that of any other university, but because at Hopkins I had created a simple life that worked. I ate, slept, got up, went to classes, went to work, studied in a library that contained more books than I could ever imagine reading, and had fun when time permitted. All my needs were met. There was nothing to worry about. Losing that simple routine and productive life in order to bring my sister Akberet to America was what worried and scared me the most. Acknowledging it made me feel selfish; it shamed me.

I had fallen in love the first time I visited the Johns Hopkins campus. I loved the Beach, and the beauty of the campus in general. It would have been painful to leave it behind, especially without completing what I had gone there to do, a mission upon which my future depended.

I woke up again from my daydream and found myself still comfortably lying on the Beach and staring up at the sky. I was exhausted. I looked at my watch and I realized I had been lying there for almost two hours. I asked myself one more time. *What can I do?*

Then, a sparkle of an idea came to me.

I might not have the money, but I surely had resources. I knew people. People had always been good to me in the past. Why not now? With that thought, I got up and started in the direction of McCoy residence hall without seeing it. I then turned around and started walking toward the Milton Eisenhower Library. I felt happy, excited, and suddenly filled with energy. At that instant I had subconsciously made up my mind to bring Akberet to the US—with the help of the people who were close to me. That decision took away my fears and anxieties and cleared all my doubts. I started looking forward to the challenge.

I started walking toward Merryman Hall, on the other end of the campus, to get to work. When I walked into the Office of Multicultural Students Affairs, I saw Rose Varner-Gaskins's office door half-open and knocked.

"Hey, stranger," Rose said.

I smiled and said, "Got a question for you. How do you bring someone to the US?"

Rose's face changed. She started looking at me as if I had done or said something wrong. She asked me if everything was okay and said I did not look right. I did not realize that the deep thinking and long hours in the sun had made me look as if I had just woken up. I brushed my hand through my tousled hair and told her everything was fine.

"It's about my sister Akberet," I said. "I need to find a way to bring her to America to get her hearing fixed."

I had told Rose about Akberet on numerous occasions. But this was the first time I mentioned that I wanted to bring her to the US.

Rose was silent for a while, thinking, and then she said, "Why don't you go to the International Students Office and ask them for a letter of support?"

"Do you know anyone over there?" I asked.

"Nick Arrindell," she told me. "He's the director."

"Will you call him for me?" I pleaded with her.

"Of course," she said.

"By the way, Rose, how come every time I asked you for information, you seem to have an answer? For someone in your position, you seem to know a whole lot of things."

"You crazy fool," she said. "Get out of my office. Go see Nick."

Rose Varner-Gaskins was born in Summerville, South Carolina. Summerville, affectionately known to its residents as Flower Town USA, is a small town twenty-six miles west of Charleston. Rose was raised in a warm, loving, and caring family and was nurtured by neighbors and her church community. Faith in God was a central part of her family life. Her parents were very active in a Wesley United Methodist Church, where her father was a deacon. As a deacon, her father would often go house to house to give communion to sick and elderly church members, and Rose would accompany him.

During Rose's youth, the social climate was riddled with problems, and many of those problems were discussed at the Varners' dining table. Discussions often centered on social issues, and on the involvement of the National Association for the Advancement of Colored People on those issues locally as well as nationally. Rose's oldest sister would rise to leadership in the NAACP. The family discussed their concerns for her safety and the safety of others working in the civil rights movement (called the Movement) during those days. At a young age, Rose learned that families had to sacrifice safety if they were to be leaders in the fight for racial equality.

Rose often met and interacted with civil rights leaders because of her sister's work. Rose's first personal attempt at activism came at age eleven, when a group of marchers came through her town and she decided to participate. As part of the day's events, a sit-in was staged at a local eatery. But when police were called to the scene, Rose fled with some of the other kids for fear of getting into trouble. A year later, Rose and her two sisters went into a drugstore in downtown Charleston, where they were not allowed to sit down to eat. One of Rose's sisters, who could pass for white, went into the drugstore and sat down to eat while Rose and her other sister watched from the window. The sisters thought they had truly accomplished something. Approximately two weeks later, however, the sisters were awakened by noise outside and found a burning cross on their front lawn.

When it came to academics, Rose was bright and energetic and performed well from elementary through high school. Yet Rose's school experiences were marred with loneliness and experiences of not fitting in. When she was in the second grade, one day during recess a schoolyard bully threatened to beat up any kid who played with Rose. Rose was really white, the bully said, and if anyone dared to play with her, they would get beat up after school. As a result, Rose was ostracized for the next two years, and she spent much of that time indoors with teachers, but neither Rose nor any of the other kids told their parents or teachers what was going on.

When the US Congress passed the Civil Rights Act in July of 1964, ending school segregation, Rose and one of her sisters went to Summerville High. There she found herself again eating lunch alone, being teased by kids because she was black, and being laughed at by many of her classmates. Almost as soon as she began classes, one classmate dropped his pencil on the floor. Rose made the mistake of picking it up and attempting to hand it to him, but he declined to touch it after she had done so.

Rose graduated from high school in 1970. Given their strong emphasis on educational accomplishment, the family assumed that she would go straight to college, but to their shock Rose had other plans. Over their strenuous objections, Rose married her high school sweetheart a week after she graduated and started a family shortly thereafter. Rose and her husband opened a business in downtown Charleston, the first black family to do so. The black community in particular rallied around the young couple. However, business being business, the young family still needed a stable income, so Rose applied for and was offered a position at the local college as a roving secretary—one who moved from department to department, filling in for other employees for short periods of time. Two days before arriving to begin work, Rose received a phone call from the person who interviewed her stating that a mistake had been made and that someone else would be filling the position.

Later that same day, Rose received another call from the equal employment opportunity/affirmative action officer for the college. This person had challenged the hire of the other candidate, whose qualifications were not a match for Rose's, and told Rose to report to work as originally planned. At this point, Rose really did not want the position, but the salary was good, so she took it. She thrived in the job. Her responsibilities quickly grew, and this enhanced her confidence. By the time Rose had been there for five years, she had worked in the Xerox center, the continuing education center, the counseling center, and the office of the dean of undergraduate studies. Each new assignment brought greater responsibility, which made it easy to advance from the secretarial to the administrative arena. Her first administrative promotion was as a staff assistant in the dean's office. She was sent for training that included conferences, seminars, and workshops. Years later Rose would recognize that the relationship she shared with her director, the dean, was a mentor/mentee relationship. Were it not for him, Rose does not think she would have realized her potential later on, nor would she have gained the foundation of confidence that helped her develop as an administrator.

The provost at the college appointed her the foreign student adviser. In that role, Rose further developed a host family program the former adviser for international students had established and developed a direct exchange program with Grenoble University in France. She later traveled all over the United States for training and to attend exchange conferences with coordinators from member universities with student exchange programs.

While attending one of these conferences in the Washington, DC, area, where some of her family now lived, Rose met her second husband. They got married five years later and she moved to Columbia, Maryland. Leaving her home in South Carolina was difficult, since by this time, her mom had already been diagnosed with Alzheimer's disease.

It took Rose six months to find a position at George Washington University. Although her résumé was a testament to superior abilities and varied experiences at the administrative level, Rose found herself repeatedly explaining the irony of working in an educational setting as an administrator without an advanced degree. She finally settled on a support position. During the six months that she worked as an administrative assistant, she received training in several software applications that helped when she was promoted to the position of educational opportunity program assistant. The difficulty in finding a position that matched her experience and knowledge, and having to repeatedly prove her skills, made Rose realize that she needed to do for herself what she had helped so many students do before: complete her degree.

She began again taking classes. Since her job often required her to work at night, she could only take one or two classes each semester.

Rose got to Johns Hopkins University when one of her directors left GW to take a new position and Rose joined her there as a program coordinator. Rose's duties at Hopkins's Office of Multicultural Students Affairs included organizing, developing and presenting leadership, orientation, and diversity workshops for students, advising student organizations, and offering nontherapeutic counseling.

At the time we had this conversation, Rose was looking forward to the day when she would be able to include her degree in introductions when facilitating workshops. In the meantime, Rose gave credit for all she had to overcome and had accomplished to having had a strong spiritual foundation, a strong supportive family, and encouraging and supportive work environments.

The next day, Rose spoke to Nick Arrindell to see if there was a way he could help. She told me that he would be willing to talk to me.

When I explained the details of my situation to Dr. Arrindell, he suggested the possibility of a B-2 (visitor's) visa for my sister. He gave me an affidavit form and said that he'd be happy to write me a letter of support.

By the end of November, I had all the necessary documents in hand: letters of employment verification from the Homewood Academic Computing and the Office of Multicultural Students Affairs, the completed affidavit, and the letter of support from Dr. Arrindell. I notarized all the paperwork and sent it to my parents. The documents arrived in Asmara by the first week of December. My dad, who had just returned to Eritrea in 1994 after living in exile for fifteen years, received the documents.

When I called home to find out the status of Akberet's visa application, my dad told me it had been rejected. I asked for the reason the embassy gave them, but my dad said he did not understand the reason for the rejection. He asked me to come and talk to the American consulate in Eritrea. I told him that was not possible. My dad tried to convince me that if I were to come and talk to them in person, they would somehow issue Akberet a visa.

I finally said, "Even if I wanted to come, I couldn't before the end of the semester! I have final exams."

After a silence that seemed to last forever, my dad said in a defeated tone, "Do whatever your heart tells you, son."

This was a tactic my parents had often used on me. I hated that tone. I hated the phrase "whatever your heart tells you." In other words, my dad was saying, "You are disobeying me, but you must know better." My dad knew what my heart was telling me. I had told him what my mind was telling me. I knew what my heart had been telling me since Thursday, September 14, 1989, the day I left home. It had been telling me to go back. I didn't want to listen to my heart, because my mind had other plans. I wanted to listen to my head. Finally, I gave in. I decided to do what my parents wanted.

Actually, I am not sure whether the weight of my dad's words swayed my decision or whether I used him to do something I had not had the courage to do for many years. I had been away from home for so long that, without even realizing it, I had started to doubt if I would ever go back. My communications with old friends at home had started to wane. I was so overwhelmed with my new life, school, and work in America that I barely had time to even write those letters anymore. I had been an avid correspondent, sending my frequent letters to friends with people who were traveling to Eritrea. My friends also wrote back often. But once I started college, I barely had time to write. Looking back now, I truly believe that I went to Eritrea because I was homesick rather than because I believed I could make the consular officers change their minds about Akberet's visa.

Otherwise, why wouldn't I have consulted Professor Tekie Fessehatzion, my local confidant and trusted friend, instead of rushing away with no word to anyone? Even worse, I kept Afewerki and Eden in the dark. I just could not find words to tell anyone why I was departing so suddenly and neglecting my exams.

I had wanted to tell Professor Tekie, but I knew he would say and do whatever he could to stop me from "messing up" my life, as he told me afterward. He advised me relentlessly to support myself before I could think about helping others. His philosophy, with which I fully agree, was simple and direct: "If you cannot stand on your own feet, you will not be able to provide support to others."

Whether it was because I didn't want to let my parents down or that I used my parents as an excuse to fulfill my dream of returning home, I decided to go to Eritrea without any plan for how to accomplish my objective, a goal that did not have any clarity. I bought a plane ticket to fly to Eritrea on Saturday, December 31, 1994.

I took three of my exams a week early (during the reading/ study period). I arranged with my professors to take the other two exams, in linear algebra and cell biology, after I got back. With a "positive delusion" under my belt, I left Baltimore on New Year's Eve and arrived in Asmara on Sunday, the next day. On Tuesday, January 3, my dad, Akberet, and I went to the US Embassy. We were told to come back the following Thursday. On that second visit, for reasons I did not understand then— and will never fully understand—the consular officer gave Akberet the visa. The only unfulfilled requirement was that we obtain a letter of clearance from Amanuel Elementary, Akberet's school, stating that the family did not owe any fees, allowing her to get an exit visa from Eritrea. Since Amanuel was my old school and I had left in good standing, the principal was very helpful in expediting the process.

My parents dipped into their savings and—to my profound relief, as that was another part of the puzzle I had not solved—came up with the fourteen thousand birr (which at the time was equivalent to $1,500 US) needed for airfare.

On January 14, 1995, I came back to the US with Akberet in my charge. I took my linear algebra and cell biology exams that same week, thanks to the generosity and flexibility of my professors.

Akberet had an initial medical examination with Dr. Jack Dalton, who recommended that she see at least two specialists in ear surgery to determine the likelihood of recovering her hearing. Jack suggested one doctor from Hopkins and one from the University of Maryland. I knew I would not be able to pay for a second opinion, so I told Jack that I would be more than happy to accept whatever procedure the Hopkins doctor recommended. Jack contacted the office of a Dr. Michael Holiday, an otolaryngologist—head and neck surgeon—and set up an appointment.

The results of a CT scan showed that Akberet's hearing loss was due to a lack of treatment and care at the early stages of an ear infection, which had led to a skin growth known as cholesteatoma in the middle of her left ear, behind the eardrum. The infection, coupled with the tumor, gradually spread and destroyed both eardrums.

Dr. Holiday suggested Akberet have surgery to remove the tumor, which, if not removed as soon as possible, would result in further damage to her ear's internal membrane and, ultimately, affect her nervous system. After the tumor was removed, surgeries for an eardrum replacement could proceed.

Thanks to credit cards and free balance transfers, I was able to cover the expenses for the CT scan and other examinations. However, when Dr. Holiday's office informed me that I would need a deposit of at least $8,000 for the tumor removal surgery, I asked him to hold off on the surgery schedule until I came up with either the money needed or a payment plan. I started looking for ways of getting Akberet into the National Institutes of Health or the John Hopkins Medical Institute, where they might be able to perform the surgery as part of their research programs.

I asked immigrant medical students for help, hoping they could get her into a program. But based on my sister's age and legal status in the US (fifteen years old with a B-2 visitor's visa), I could not open any door for her treatment. As a last resort, my adviser and I decided that the best thing to do would be for me to take a year off from school and get a full-time job to earn the money required for the surgeries. I also went to see Professor Tekie Fessehatzion and discussed the option I had considered. Unfortunately, it did not take much effort for Professor Tekie to pinpoint the fallacy in my grand option.

"Do you have a job lined up?" he asked.

I just stared at him. I had, of course, not been thinking linearly. I told him, without any confidence, that I would start looking for a job immediately. He gave me a fatherly look and told me to find a job before I considered withdrawing from school. He said he was willing to help me explore other options, but he would not embrace any plan that had to do with withdrawing from school. From his tone, I sensed the topic of withdrawal was not to be raised with him again. I obliged.

I then started searching for any funding that John Hopkins Hospital might have for emergency medical treatment. After several months of looking, I was able to get a phone number for such an office.

After an examination of the facts, the hospital approved the tumor removal as an emergency case. The hospital assured Dr. Holiday's office that they would cover the surgical expenses, and as a result, Akberet had her first surgery for the removal of the cholesteatoma tumor on August 31, 1995, and I did not have to leave school.

Akberet's second surgery took place on March 5, 1996. As a result of the surgeries, Akberet was able to regain 80 percent of her hearing.

Within three years, Akberet passed her General Education Development (GED) test. She then earned an associate degree in 2001, followed by a bachelor's degree in management information systems.

She would later marry a wonderful young man named Kehase Beyene and become the mother of two great kids, Lidya and Nathaniel.

After exploring multiple majors and taking many courses in different areas of study at Hopkins, I finished my course work in December 1996, a semester earlier than my graduation on May 22, 1997. I'd come to Hopkins intending to major in electrical and computer engineering. I lasted in the computer science department for a semester and decided to change to premed in the middle of my freshman year. After discussing my interest in mathematics and physics with a number of students on campus and still leaving open my options for going to medical school, I decided to join the department of biophysics. Incidentally, starting my sophomore year, I was assigned to support the department of biophysics as a student computer consultant. I was providing support to the various mainframe-based FORTRAN and Pascal-based applications the department was using for data modeling. I also ended up working at Dr. Warner Love's lab for two and half years, gathering data to determine the three-dimensional structure of hemoglobin using X-ray crystallography.

After I completed my course work, my student consultant post at Homewood Academic Computing was converted to a full-time customer support position, providing support to the Hopkins communities both on and off campus. But as much as I loved and enjoyed every minute of my life at Hopkins, I knew it had to end.

Thus, I started frequenting the career counseling office. While going through the recruiter list the career counseling office maintained, I was told Bloomberg was coming to campus to interview candidates.

I figured I had nothing to lose. I thought the experience would give me an idea of what to expect when I later went to other interviews. I filled the generic employment application form and waited for the interviewers. I was relaxed, confident, and ready to learn.

The first part of the interview was with Ken Cooper, at the time head of the company's internal systems group.

Ken started with basic questions related to the overall software development life cycle, starting from requirements elicitation, design, algorithm writing, debugging techniques, and documentation. I did not have any difficulty answering Ken's questions, considering the experience I had gained from the four years I spent working at Johns Hopkins.

Then Ken asked me three questions I did not expect. He started with a scenario. He said to assume that I had a final project that I must pass in order to graduate. Unfortunately, the software application I developed for the project would not work. I would try to fix the bug many times, but the software still would not work. Finally, I made some changes to the source code and tried the application again. This time the application would work, even though I did not know how the changes I made to the code had contributed to the outcome. Based on this scenario, Ken's question was, would I turn in my assignment, considering the application had worked despite the fact that I did not understand why it was working?

Life at Johns Hopkins

I answered the first question flat out: "No!" Ken asked a few more questions concerning why I would not consider my project complete without fully understanding how it was working. I consistently replied that the application could have worked for many reasons, but not for the reasons I knew. Since I did not know why or how it worked, I would not consider the assignment finished. I expressed my view freely and with confidence, since I was fairly certain that I was not going to get the job anyway. My primary objective for the interview was simply to get the experience. But would I have answered the question differently had I gone to the interview with a goal of getting hired? I do not know, but I seriously doubt it.

The various computer science classes I had taken and the three-plus years I worked on campus had prepared me for these types of software engineering questions. From his line of questioning, Ken was trying to understand to what extent I valued software reliability, the probability of a given application returning consistent results within a defined environment. Software reliability has a direct impact on the overall system's reliability. As I learned later, this is of vital importance to Bloomberg, because the company provides highly complex trading systems and financial data that needs to be presented with utmost reliability, allowing its customers to make informed decisions.

The second question was simpler: What would I do if I found a printer out of paper?

I replied quickly—if I found a printer out of paper I would either reload the tray, if there was paper available, or find someone who could help me get some paper. Ken just nodded without saying anything. I did not understand what he was trying to get from the second question. That is probably why I never forgot it in the years to come.

While working at K/B movie theaters and in the various divisions of Johns Hopkins University, I encountered people of various outlooks on and attitudes toward specific tasks. At the movie theater, selling tickets and attending the concession stands were everyone's first choices, followed by picking up the trash from the auditoriums. No one liked cleaning and restocking the bathrooms. Tasks related to sweeping and mopping the floors and tending to bathroom supplies were done either by turns or by newbies. I honestly did not care much about what I did—my main focus was on getting the work done as soon as I could so I could hide behind the stairs to the projection booth and start my homework. Tending the bathrooms and cleaning the auditoriums were the two tasks that took the least amount of time. I did not have to wait for the manager to ask me to get one or both of these tasks done.

At Hopkins, my main interest was to learn. I did practically everything I could to learn about the various technologies in use. I visited a number of professors' and students' residences to help them with their issues related to hardware and software or dial-up internet connectivity. Sometimes their problems could be solved by something as simple as rebooting their machines.

The last question was very easy to answer as well. Ken asked, "What was your favorite class at Johns Hopkins?"

I didn't even have to think about that. I had just finished the course. It was New Technologies and International Development, a sociology class I took in my final semester.

The class was taught by Professor Patricia Fernández-Kelly, a distinguished research scientist who specializes in migration and global economic development. Don't get me wrong—I enjoyed most of my classes at Hopkins. The difference is that what I learned in calculus, differential equations, linear algebra, advanced and intermediate physics, physical chemistry, computer science, and the rest of the sciences were merely tools that helped me to understand and analyze logical, conceptually tangible ideas. Professor Fernández-Kelly's class, in comparison, challenged my outlook on life.

When I joined Professor Fernández-Kelly's class in September 1996, my outlook on my environment was like a typical member of a highly consumerist society. I never paid much attention to how the gadgets I was using were made or delivered. I simply admired, enjoyed, and of course hoped to get better ones at a cheaper price, soon. I was fascinated by the newly released high-performance SGI Indigo computer servers we obtained when I was working at Homewood Academic Computing. Installing and configuring a Windows operating system on a PowerPC (also known as PowerMac) and trying to understand how the system managed memory and partitions was fascinating for anyone involved in technology at the time. Thanks to the individuals and institutions providing funding to Hopkins, we had access to cutting-edge technological innovations, especially in the field of information technology. I was working with the teams rolling out new technologies. I enjoyed every bit of it. I enjoyed technology so much, I spent many nights at my desk in the Homewood Academic Computing lab even when I was not on duty.

Throughout my years at Hopkins, or before, I never paid attention to the process of technological advancement. I only enjoyed it. As time went, I had become part of the privileged few, and I didn't even know it. Professor Fernández-Kelly's class exposed us to the human cost of technological advancement. Eric Wolf's *Europe and the People Without History* and Aldous Huxley's *Brave New World* were but two of the many challenging and highly enlightening assigned books that contributed to my new perspective in Professor Fernández-Kelly's class.

At five that same afternoon, I received an email with a job offer from Bloomberg. The formal offer, in the form of a contract, arrived via FedEx a few days later. I moved to New York City to join the ten-week Bloomberg new-hire training program on June 2, 1997, ten days after my graduation from Hopkins.

To take a break from the Bloomberg new-hire training boot camp, on Saturday, August 30, 1997, I went to the Eritrean Community Center located at West 125th Street in Harlem to celebrate September 1, the start of the armed struggle for Eritrea's independence. I went there with the family of Genet and Beraki Yebio Kelib. The celebration started around seven p.m., and by nine the music was at its peak. After dancing for a couple of rounds, I went to the bar and asked the young man who was going back and forth behind the counter for a can of soda. He appeared to be my age. He stared at me for few minutes, and before handing me my soda, he said, "Is your name Dawit?" I responded affirmatively. "Is your father's name Gebremichael?" the guy continued. Again I nodded affirmatively. "Did you grow up in Gejeret?"

At that point, I thought it was time for me to start asking the questions. "Do we know each other?" I said, and he started smiling. "Oh, my God! Is that you, Daniel Abraha Tesfay?" When he smiled, I saw the fracture on one of his upper teeth and immediately realized who he was—one of my best friends from childhood.

I knew Daniel left to join the EPLF and made it safely to independence, but New York City was the last place I expected to see him. We hugged and spoke briefly while the celebratory Eritrean music was playing at a deafening volume. I took my soda and went back to my seat, promising Daniel I would be back to catch up.

At the end of the party and once we finished cleaning up the Eritrean Community Center, around six Sunday morning, Daniel and I went to Floridita, a Latin American restaurant located a block away, ordered breakfast, and started to summarize the eight years we'd spent in separate parts of the world. Daniel did most of the talking, of course, and I listened attentively with very little interruption, asking him about our friends and their whereabouts. Daniel has a photographic memory and is an amazingly gifted storyteller.

"You know, a lot of things changed in Asmara after you left," Daniel said. "About a year after you left, Simon Tedros Gebru, Efrem Semere Teklit, and I left to the field to join the Popular Front," he said, referring to the Eritrean People's Liberation Front.

Simon Tedros Gebru lived across from our house, Efrem Semere Teklit lived in the third house north of us, and Daniel Abraha Tesfay lived in the fourth house south of us.

"How did you manage to get out of Asmara with all the checkpoints surrounding the city?"

"We were able to get our IDs once we turned fifteen, and we purchased the travel permits from a guy who was able to steal sealed letters and put our names on each letter for our travel permit. We paid the guy two hundred birr each," Daniel continued.

The remnants of war—unexploded ordnance—left in Eritrea

I asked Daniel the whereabouts of the neighborhood kids, most of whom I had not heard from for many years, and we got to Adey Ma'aza and Adey Mehret, who affectionately referred me as "my nephew" every time I went to buy *suwa* (a traditional fermented alcoholic drink brewed from sorghum) when our family members visited from the villages.

"Adey Ma'aza was once arrested by the Ethiopian security and was taken to the Fifth Precinct police station for interrogation," Daniel continued. "One of the investigators at the police station asked Adey Ma'aza to 'confess her sins and come clean at her own accord.' When she told the interrogator there was no sin she knew of, she was put in a solitary confinement for three days. At the end of the third day, the same interrogator took her out of her confinement for further interrogation and decided to question her about the 'sinful crime' she supposedly had committed. The interrogation told Adey Ma'aza that she was accused of serving suwa to a *Sha'bia wonbedie* [a bandit, member of the EPLF]. The witty Adey Ma'aza told the interrogator that she might have done it considering she would even serve a dog with her best suwa if the interrogator was to send one armed with fifty cents," which was the cost of a cup of suwa at the time.

I learned later that Simon Tedros Gebru spent his youth fighting for Eritrea's independence, and he paid with his precious life defending it. Simon was martyred on May 2, 1999, during the second round of invasion at Geza-shawul (Shambqo), four months before my return to Eritrea. The second round of invasion was triggered by the Tigray People's Liberation Front, the minority group at the helm of the Ethiopian government, in the name of "border conflict."

Efrem Semere Teklit made it safely to Eritrea's independence. Both Daniel and Efrem were demobilized from the Eritrean armed forces in 1993. Efrem went back to the army and joined his unit that was stationed in the western part of Eritrea when Eritrea's survival as a nation was threatened, and he serves his country to this day.

My friendship with Daniel has since never gone more than a few days without us talking by phone.

BLOOMBERG

"How selfish so ever man may be supposed,
there are evidently some principles in his nature,
which interest him in the fortune of others, and
render their happiness necessary to him, though
he derives nothing from it, except the pleasure of
seeing it." —Adam Smith

One morning, a couple of months after I joined Bloomberg, I came to the office very early to test an application during off hours. On my way to the pantry to grab cereal and a cup of tea, I ran into none other than the CEO and founder of Bloomberg LP, Michael Bloomberg himself, in a corridor on the tenth floor. Mike stopped, glanced at me, and said, "Good morning!" As is the custom in my culture, I stood aside to let the elder man pass, without responding to his greeting. But, to my surprise, the man waited for my response. I was not sure whether to reply "Good morning" and walk away or just turn around and get back to my desk. I was shocked to see him there. I was not sure what he could be doing in the building that early in the morning. I didn't know what to say.

Finally, when I decided it would be wrong to just walk away from the CEO while expecting his paycheck at the end of the month, I said, "Good morning, sir."

He must have sensed my discomfort and nervousness, for he walked away after saying only, "Good to see you."

Forgetting why I'd gone to the pantry, I scurried back to my desk, postponing my breakfast. Out of curiosity, I accessed Bloomberg's proprietary internal directory, where employees are able to view the status of their colleagues in real time. The tool displays detailed information of Bloomberg staff, including the date and time the employee logged in (or logged out), in which Bloomberg office the employee logged in, and details about the employee's contacts and departmental information. The directory showed that the CEO had come to the office at 6:23 that morning. That was one of my early lessons in work ethic at Bloomberg, and I decided to follow suit.

For my first annual performance review, I was sitting alone in one of the Bloomberg conference rooms at 499 Park Avenue in Manhattan. Floor-to-ceiling glass windows enclosed the room on three sides. The wall across from the door was the only solid one, and it featured a large screen displaying the latest headlines reported by Bloomberg News.

During my year at Bloomberg, I had heard much talk of the company's strong performance-based incentives for its employees. According to the grapevine, Bloomberg's reward system was used to motivate and encourage employees from the bottom up. But now it was my turn to get my first year's performance evaluated, and hopefully rewarded. It was mid-April 1998, and I was waiting for Ken Cooper, my manager, to come from human resources with the necessary forms. I sat there thinking about the company and wondering how my first year would be appraised.

Ken entered the conference room with my appraisal forms and placed them on the table between us. He sat next to me and started going through the numbers. I really had no idea what those numbers meant, though he tried to explain to me the way Bloomberg's performance-based certificates worked. The few numbers I still remember are the 0.33 percent of the number of terminals sold within the appraisal period, multiplied by the number of certificates awarded at the beginning of the year, plus some additional factors that made up an employee's annual bonus. Ken went on and on, discussing subject matter I did not understand, until finally he said the words I had been waiting for since our meeting began.

"That will increase your compensation package for next year by 30 percent. Congratulations." I was speechless. I did not know what to say except "Thank you." I was out of words. The raise was much more than I'd anticipated. I would easily have settled for a 5 to 10 percent raise in compensation. With that, I was fired up and ready to do even more for the company.

After working at Bloomberg for about a year and half, at the end of 1998, I requested personal leave to go see my mom, who was sick at the time, and flew home to Asmara.

During the short period of time I stayed in Asmara, I discussed the development and application of information technology in the developing world with several old friends and some new acquaintances. Just before I left to return to the US, I was approached by Ezana Negusse Rozario, a young graduate assistant who had become one of my new acquaintances, to give a presentation on IT and its applications at Asmara University. I was reluctant, telling him point-blank that I was just out of college and would be the least qualified to talk about the subject in public. But Ezana was persistent and told me there would be barely ten or fifteen people in attendance, and that they would be undergraduate students. With that understanding, I gave in and accepted his offer.

To my surprise when I arrived that night, the hall was filled with close to a hundred students, both graduate and undergraduate, as well as a number of professors. I started off nervously but did what I had to do: I relied on my four years' experience in technical support at Hopkins and less than two years' experience at Bloomberg to deliver a presentation that lasted about thirty minutes, then I opened the floor for discussions. When I heard questions coming directly from the topics I had raised during the presentation, I was shocked at the degree to which they had been paying attention. I had been struggling to get to the end of the presentation, fearing that I was making a fool of myself, especially as the room had been so quiet throughout my remarks that you could have heard a pin drop.

I pivoted and I told the audience I thought it would be beneficial if we all discussed the topics and questions together, so that we could learn from each other. I told them that

I would moderate the discussion. The presentation that had been scheduled to last one hour turned into a roundtable that lasted close to four hours.

The presentation at Asmara University was a powerful experience that was to shape the course of the next several years of my life. It brought me closer to the society I had been born into and in touch with how the material I had been studying for so long might contribute to its betterment.

I brought back with me what I had learned from the presentation at Asmara University, and I started working on a plan to develop a significant and sustainable knowledge transfer between the Eritreans at home and Eritrean expatriates in the US.

The objective was simple and the vision was clear: How can the people of Eritrea take ownership of information technology and claim it as theirs by taking it one step farther, the same way Europeans claimed the advancement of mathematics by creating calculus out of algebra, which they borrowed from the Arabs?[35] I wanted Eritreans to use information technology to accomplish the objectives they set for themselves, by themselves, executing their own vision.

I knew that the gap between this vision and my capabilities was as stark as day and night. But I also knew that in any endeavor the first step is the most crucial. And if I put all my energies into the first step, I might get somewhere.

I thought I could discuss my idea with Michael Bloomberg, because I knew that he had a history of backing innovative projects that included supporting Johns Hopkins University, his alma mater.

35 The term is derived from Arabic, *al-jabr*, meaning "reunion of broken parts."

In preparation, I needed to know as much as I could about Bloomberg the man, not the CEO. I asked a few of my colleagues what they knew about him, and Harry Surden, my team leader, directed me to a book that Mike had written about his life, called *Bloomberg on Bloomberg*. I immediately purchased a copy and began to study. The following passage in the book made a great impression on me and encouraged me to pursue my idea farther:

> "Asking for money is difficult and distasteful. But unpleasant as it is, you have two choices: do not ask and do not help as much as you can, or ask and maximize assistance to your favorite causes. Do you care enough to swallow your pride, summon up your courage, commit your resources, and take the time to pick up the phone? Those who do follow through do not necessarily find it easier than those who cannot bear to make the call—they just care more about helping."

This passage forced me to face my "poor man's mentality." For fear of offending someone or saying something foolish, a poor man fears speaking, though he may possibly have something important to contribute. Excessive caution tells a poor man to remain silent. The poor evaluate and reevaluate their thoughts before speaking them. A poor man has four eyes: the two that help him to see his surroundings and the two that are always staring back at him.

After all my pondering, I decided to go ahead and talk to Mike Bloomberg. As I prepared for my appointment, I considered which of the two newspaper articles that had been written about me to give to Mike as background information. The Johns Hopkins newsletter, *The Gazette*, of May 19, 1997, had featured an article titled "Good as Gold." *USA Today* also published an article on me, titled "An Arduous Trek to Graduation," on May 22, 1997. I decided on the Hopkins paper, because I knew Mike was a Hopkins alumnus and benefactor, as well as then chairman of the university's board of trustees.

On my first visit to his desk (like every other employee at Bloomberg LP, he did not have an office), I gave Mike a summary of my idea, a map of Eritrea, and the following story from *The Gazette*.

Good as Gold

It was on a Thursday in September 1989 that Habte, then only fourteen, left his home in Eritrea, Africa, with his older sister and his sister-in-law. Together they walked for two months to Kenya so he could escape being drafted into the Ethiopian army during his country's vicious war for independence from Ethiopia.

It was another Thursday when he was freed from a Kenyan jail after months of being imprisoned for illegal entry into Kenya. After working as a bus conductor and teaching himself English by reading Agatha Christie and Charles Dickens novels with a translating dictionary, it was on a Thursday that, with the sponsorship of a Silver Spring church, Habte and his two sisters left Africa for America.

And this Thursday, Habte graduates from Hopkins.

Seeing his father is especially emotional, says Habte, because since 1989, he has only seen him once, very briefly, when he went to Eritrea to retrieve Akberet.

His father had been a member of the Eritrean Liberation Front. In 1979, one of his comrades was captured by the Ethiopian forces and, to avoid torture, fingered Habte's father as an ELF leader. His father managed to escape to Saudi Arabia, where he worked as a truck driver and sent money to provide for the family. Two years ago, when Eritrea was officially declared independent, his father was finally reunited with his family.

When Habte graduates Thursday, his father will watch his son receive his diploma. Somewhere along his journey, Habte learned he doesn't have to be a doctor to heal.

And although he doesn't rule out medical school, he's beginning to think maybe it is not what he will end up doing. His real love is computer programming. At the end of this month he will move to New York City to take a job as a programmer at Bloomberg Business News.

The most important thing, he has learned, is taking care of family and to remember those who have cut him breaks along the way: the high school counselor who made Habte apply for the scholarship; the church which paid for his first flight to America; Jack Dalton, the local internist and mentor who guided Habte through the foreign, complicated health care system; and his advisers here at Hopkins.

"And I think we, mankind, have to go through hardships, which test our fortitude, courage, spirit and integrity as gold is tested by fire."[36]

---

36 "Good as Gold," *The Gazette*. May 19, 1997.

Mike asked me what group I worked with and the name of my manager. He told me he would speak with Ken Cooper and get back to me.

A week later I followed up with Mike and learned that Ken had told him I was one of his great programmers. Mike said he would hate to lose me. I thanked him for the compliment and for his confidence in me. Mike admitted that he knew very little about Eritrea and asked me to describe my country and its economic outlook. I tried to paint a decent picture.

I told Mike that Eritrea had recently become a new country after a lengthy war for independence and that, as such, there was no real economy to speak of. Everything was starting from scratch. After listening patiently, he asked me to give him something in writing. I had not prepared anything because I had thought, based on my reading of his book, that he would not appreciate any unnecessarily lengthy documentation.

Mike said, "Come on, give me some kind of business plan."

I went back and referred to his book. Apparently, he had not said, "Don't write a business plan." What he'd said was: "Think logically and passionately about what you'd like to do. Work out all steps of the process—the entire what, when, where, why, and how. Then, sit down after you are absolutely positive you know it cold, and write it out."

Bloomberg's openness, transparency, and merit-based reward system are also but a few of the company's features that allow the institution to get the best from each of us. Because of Bloomberg's willingness to support important causes, I felt like this was my opportunity to show him the situation in Eritrea and get his support. Personally, working for Bloomberg felt like working for my favorite philanthropy. I found Bloomberg to be the largest and the most efficiently run philanthropic business.

Three months later I gave Mike the following business plan.

Executive Summary:

For the industrial economies of the world, the balance between knowledge and resources has shifted in favor of the former. Knowledge has become the most important determinant of standard of living, three-fourths more important than land, labor, and tools. Today's technologically advanced economies are knowledge based. The lesson for the developing economies is clear: they have to acquire and use knowledge if they do not want to be left behind. Unfortunately knowledge cannot be bought off the shelf. It has to be created and/or adapted for a specific purpose. Developing countries have to increase their capacity to use knowledge, to invest in education, and to take advantage of new technologies for acquiring and disseminating knowledge. This is where NATNA Business Solutions comes in.

The idea of forming NATNA Business Solutions emanated from the recognition of the growing need for professional software engineers with expertise in information technology. The dependency on software is growing rapidly; unfortunately, the number of skilled IT workers in Eritrea has not been able to keep up with the rapid growth. This drastic shortage of qualified software developers and IT personnel is forcing American companies operating in emerging economies to depend heavily on offshore consulting and software development firms. When outsourcing development projects, companies worldwide look for IT solutions that are of the highest quality, lowest cost, and most adaptable in the face of changing circumstances. NATNA's investment will be in training IT professionals and utilizing them to meet the competitive demands of a global IT market.

NATNA Business Solutions will be an enterprise based in Eritrea, providing technical training to the local market and business software solutions to clients worldwide. Eritrea is chosen as a base because, unlike many countries that went through a similar experience (a long, armed struggle for independence) that left their economic and financial structures destroyed, Eritrea retains a singular determination to utilize the marketplace for growth, a commitment to start afresh in search of new ideas and practices to rebuild its economy.

What makes this initiative different from those of other technological firms is that NATNA seeks to establish a strong, vital relationship with the Eritrean economic landscape. NATNA's plan to export locally developed software parallels the Eritrean government's export-oriented microeconomic policy. As an organization of highly skilled developers, NATNA could deliver customized software solutions to compete in the global market. Its local presence would entail recruiting and training Eritrean professionals who would be able to build products suitable for these broader markets, while narrowing the gap between Eritrea and the rest of the world. Clients throughout Africa would be able to make the transition into the information technology age with ease due to the proximity and availability of technical training for their employees. This would result in increased productivity and competitiveness while reducing overall development and maintenance costs for both domestic and international companies operating in the region.

Natna is a Tigrinya word that stands for "ours," and I picked that name because I wanted everyone associated with the project to have ownership in what they were going to produce. I cannot continue without mentioning the tremendous assistance and support I received from my great friend Sewit Tekeste Ahderom, whom I met while we both were in college. Sewit went to the University of Connecticut in Storrs, and in those years Sewit and I helped manage many Eritrea-related internet relay chat rooms during our spare time.

The rest of the business plan dealt with basic market analysis and the standard software development life cycle: project initiation, requirements analysis, design, and development.

Mike told me he would read the business plan on a trip to London, and to check with him when he got back. I thought that was a great thing—seven to eight hours in flight was the most valuable time I could have asked from Mike.

When Mike got back, it was clear that he had read the plan, and his comment to me was, "Listen, I don't think this is feasible, but if you are willing to invest your time to help others, I can help you with money and anything you need from the company. When you make a lot of money, build a hospital or something that could help people." While I was sitting in the conference room across from him, Mike picked up the phone and asked the operator to connect him to Marty Geller. He spoke with someone at Marty Geller's office and informed the person on the other end of the phone to work with me on getting the initial seed capital.

Mike's words seemed to echo the words of Kahlil Gibran, the great Lebanese American philosopher:

> "There are those who give and know not pain in giving, nor do they seek joy, nor give with mindfulness of virtue; they give as in yonder valley the myrtle breathes its fragrance into space. Through the hands of such as these God speaks, and from behind their eyes. He smiles upon the earth."[37]

Unlike those financially fortunate individuals who try relentlessly to have their faces seen in every quarter of New York City, Mike Bloomberg seemed to represent Gibran's ideal philanthropist. With his support and encouragement, Mike removed the extra pair of eyes that were always staring inward at me. I became a man with only two eyes again, the two eyes I was born with.

---

37   Gibran, Kahlil. *The Prophet.* New York: Alfred A. Knopf, 1923.

Now that the proposal was done and the high-level vision and road map defined and put on paper, it was time to turn to the fundamentals and identify the first steps in actually getting to the vision. A concrete project was needed.

I contacted Yemane Tesfay, the general manager of Commercial Bank of Eritrea, and sent him a proposal to automate the CBE's banking operations. Yemane's positive response to our proposal was encouraging.

I flew out of Washington, DC, on August 10, 1999, and arrived at Asmara International Airport the next morning around one a.m. My parents picked me up from the airport around three a.m. and we got home in a mere fifteen minutes. My mom brought a dish with some onions and green pepper, as the tradition dictates, in order to help me adapt to the change of environment. We also had tea, and by the time we decided to go to bed it was already four. To avoid jet lag, I decided to read for the rest of the morning.

Around five in the morning, I heard some noise outside and went out to check what it was. I saw my youngest sister, Tigisti, walking out of the bathroom. Tigisti saw me and said good morning. I replied, saying good morning, and asked her what she was doing this early in the morning. Tigisti asked, "Didn't you know?" and started to walk away. I was a bit surprised and asked her what she meant. What was I supposed to have known when I just got home from years in exile? After we exchanged a few words, I told her that I was serious and that she needed to tell me whatever it was she thought I knew unless she wanted me to wake up my parents and ask them. Tigisti finally came out and told me that our sister Simret was in the hospital. Tigisti then went to prepare food for us to take to the hospital for Simret.

A few minutes later, my parents got up and my dad came to the living room and filled me in. Apparently, Simret had been in the hospital for more than two weeks. She had been wounded by Ethiopian artillery on the southern (Assab) front. Eritrea and Ethiopia were still fighting over the border, even after independence.

My parents, Tigisti, and I went to Halibet Hospital around six thirty in the morning. The guard at the hospital let us into the compound, and my parents led us to Ward M. I was shocked to see one of Simret's feet on a stretcher. We exchanged greetings and I asked her what had happened. She briefly told me that it was nothing; she was just hit by a mortar fragment on the hip. I was shocked and surprised with Simret's nonchalant and casual way of describing her situation. But, then, seeing the number of wounded soldiers and the type of injuries most had sustained, Simret's just "a mortar hit on the hip" was just that.

To say that I was shaken by what I was seeing in Ward M would be an understatement. "Welcome home" was all I could tell myself at the time. I was introduced to the human cost of war.

To rinse myself of what I had seen in Ward M, later that day I decided to go to the Expo compound to attend the last day of the Eritrean annual festival. I went hoping I would find something to lift me up from the depressive state I had gotten into on my first day "back home." I walked to the compound from the northern gates and started looking around.

Starting from the gate, the entire Expo compound was surrounded by so many people walking back and forth. I turned right and started walking toward the counter that had works of art displayed. I glanced at some of the displays but did not find anything of interest. I started to look around but could not find a familiar face. What a shock! I thought I pretty much knew most, if not all of Asmara's inhabitants, and yet there was no one I knew in the thousands of people surrounding me. I waited at the festival for an additional hour and finally decided to leave. There just was no point staying in yet another depressing place where there was no one I could talk to. I might as well go back to Halibet Hospital's Ward M and at least try to talk to my sister and her wounded colleagues.

I decided to take the longest route to the hospital. I needed time to recoup and think through the insurmountable challenges. I needed to clear my head. My memories of the area went all the way back to my elementary school days, when all the neighborhood kids ran cross-country on the weekends. We would start from our neighborhood in Gejeret and run all the way to our only airport and back to our neighborhood. Regardless of how long it took, each of us ran all the way to the airport and returned only after touching the pole in front of the airport entry gate. On the way to the airport, we usually took the shorter route, passing through the cement factory, the Eritrean Electric Authority, and the expo. We took the longer path on the way back. I decided to take this longer path on the way back to Halibet Hospital.

I continued my walk along the palm tree–lined sidewalks observing the variously styled one-story villas beautifying the Tiravolo neighborhood. Most of the houses were surrounded by beautifully crafted gates built with black stones separated by white paint, leaving the top third of the villa visible from outside. Some of the gates were much shorter, making the beautiful gardens inside enjoyable for people passing through the neighborhood.

When I was growing up, most of these villas were occupied by either Russian or Cuban senior military advisers or Ethiopian senior officials and their families. Our favorite childhood mischief was to ring the bells in those villas and run as fast as we could. This helped us tremendously during our cross-country races. This time, though, I was taking my time. I was in deep thought. I was confused. I felt like an outsider in my own city.

I fell in love with Asmara the day I set foot in Gejeret at a very young age. I loved my city with all of its inconsistencies and intricacies. At first, my family had to pay our dues when we came to Asmara from Adi-Hayo. It was not easy to learn the city culture and the Asmarino street talk, but we were able to pick things up fast. In a short period of time, I had become an Asmarino and joined my Asmarino friends for the rituals of initiation of those who came from the countryside after us.

This time, I felt like a newcomer. There were too many young men and women in military uniform. Some were walking alone, but most were in groups of three or more. I knew of the border war, but living in it was different than reading or hearing about it. It is never the same.

It was completely different compared to my childhood. Things appeared relatively smaller than what I was accustomed to. When I came from Adi-Hayo to Asmara, everything was humongous. Size did not matter, though. By the time I woke up from my daydream, Tiravolo was already behind me and I had reached Cambo Bolo. I stopped at the traffic light at the intersection of Warsay and Mereb Streets and I was not sure whether to go straight toward Barka High School or turn toward San Francisco Catholic Church. I turned right on Mereb Street heading toward San Francesco. After a few more turns, I saw Lateria Senai on my left side.

Standing across from Lateria Senai took me back to a bittersweet memory again. I went back to December 1985, when Lemlem and I were crossing the street on the way to our night classes at Comboni Elementary School. At the time, Lemlem was in eighth grade and I was in sixth. My dad had come from Saudi to visit us for the holidays.

I continued walking on Sematat Avenue toward Bar Folia. I walked a few steps, leaving the roundabout and the Nakfa building behind me and saw the Lancia auto parts store in front of me and the Baha'i center next. When we were young, the Baha'i center was our favorite place to visit on the way to watch a cycling race, a soccer game, or just a trip to the meat shop in Bar Folia. The Baha'i center was the only building with what we called a talking gate. We didn't know what an intercom was at the time, but we definitely knew the gate was talking every time we rang the bell. When we rang the bells of other houses, we all would run before anyone answered. It was different with the Baha'i center. We would actually wait until the gate said something—which usually was not clear—ring the bell several times more, and then run once we heard a door open inside the gate. It was fun! I was almost tempted to do it one more time for the heck of it. But then the better half of me chose to enjoy my nostalgic moment while walking toward Bar Folia.

According to Milan Kundera, the Czech-born author of the novel *Ignorance*, "the Greek word for return is *nostos*. *Algos* means suffering. So nostalgia is the suffering caused by an unappeased yearning to return." If there is an iota of accuracy to Milan Kundera's definition of nostalgia, I was truly suffering, for I very much yearned to return to that moment of my life. I wished I could.

I passed Bar Folia on my right side and reached Nyala Hotel, the tallest building in Asmara, with its legendary ten stories. I crossed the roundabout. I could have made a right turn at Bdho Avenue and passed through Cinema Croce Rossa, the best movie theater of my childhood.

Cinema Croce Rossa, as the next least expensive movie theater in Asmara, was where any kid who was able to save, collect, or borrow seventy-five cents went to watch an Indian movie. (Cinema Hamasien was the least expensive movie theater, but it was far away from our neighborhood.) Every Sunday, any passerby could see a lot of kids lined up in front of Cinema Croce Rossa, starting at nine a.m. for the movie that would start at ten. It was five or six p.m. by the time we left the movie theater. We would watch a three-hour Indian movie at least twice before we left the theater. The rest of the week, the number of fights and Indian songs in the movies we watched became the main topic of the gatherings in our neighborhood.

Instead of turning at Bdho Avenue heading toward Cinema Croce Rossa, I decided to follow Sematat Avenue and continue all the way to downtown. Passing Cinema Roma, I made a right turn at the Eritrean Telecommunications headquarters and another right turn at Harnet (Liberty) Avenue. I would have enjoyed strolling throughout Harnet Avenue any other time, but not today. My mood completely changed when I reached the building that housed the Ministry of Education. I was depressed looking at American Bar and Bar Royal across the street. I was supposed to be sitting on one of the empty chairs outside American Bar sipping cappuccino with my friends. I should have been on the mezzanine of Bar Royal drinking my favorite juice, a cocktail of orange, mango, and banana juice locally known as Spris juice. But that was not to happen. I was instead on my way to Halibet Hospital Ward M to visit those who had faced death for me to stand where I was. I was on my way to visit my heroes without knowing where the rest were. I was in an empty city with its empty streets. I was walking mindlessly. What else could I have done?

I went to the largest gathering in the city, the festival at Expo. I could not find anyone I could call by name. I walked halfway across Asmara without encountering someone I knew or who knew me. All I found were places I knew, but I was not sure if those places knew me. I started walking faster, hoping to get out of Harnet Avenue. I passed the Cathedral Catholic Church and Cinema Impero on my left side, the Municipality and Eritrean Commercial Bank on my right side, and made a right turn at Fenkil Street. I started lengthening my strides and kept walking like a zombie. I passed such neighborhoods as Monopolio and Setanta-Oto and major institutions such as the US Embassy and my alma mater Santa Anna High School without even glancing. I knew I passed through those places, because that was the only way I could get to where I was from where I started. But I had no memory of my journey from the time I made the right turn at Marsateklay Avenue till I got to Halibet Hospital. I regained my consciousness when I reached the small kiosk in front of the hospital. I bought some pieces of orange and banana and went in to Ward M.

In Ward M, a young man suddenly grabbed a crutch from under my sister Simret's bed and in Tigrinya said, "Come, sit over here," while struggling to pick himself up, using his crutch as a support. I was shocked to see this one-legged man trying to leave his seat for me and told him to sit back, that I would sit on my sister's bed. I was actually shocked to hear myself use those terms: my sister's bed. I had already started to adapt to my environment. I asked the one-legged and one-eyed young man for his name, hoping to warm up the environment. My sister answered me by saying he went by Habt'ab *wedi-Hanietay* ("the son of a warrior").

I decided to call him Hanietay, because as far as I was concerned he was a fearsome warrior who had sacrificed multiple parts of his body, irrespective of his father's repute and stature in society. I was not sure how to ask him about his leg and his eye. But I wanted to know. After contemplating for few seconds, I decided to be blunt. I said, "Hanietay, so how did you lose your eye and your leg?"

Hanietay, true to his name, nonchalantly said, "I paid my eye as a dowry for [Eritrea's] independence, and I donated my leg as a handout to the Weyane."[38] He lost his eye during the armed struggle for Eritrea's independence and his leg during

38 The original Tigrinya of the statement is provided here for readers of the language, who will understand that the meaning is very powerful and difficult to capture in translation: "ዓይነይ ገዝሚ ነጻነት ከፊለያ እግረይ ከኣንወያነ ቶኩብያ"

the Eritrea-Ethiopia border war that was ongoing. His eye for Eritrea's independence; his leg to preserve it.

I froze and stopped talking after I heard Hanietay's casual words, which were nerve-racking and humbling for someone like me, whose toughest challenge in life did not even deserve to be put on the same page as the name Hanietay.

Thanks to the conversation, I was able to gain a good grasp on my reality. My "insurmountable challenge" was not that bad at all. I just needed to readjust my perspective, and I did.

From a business perspective, when I first arrived in Eritrea, the challenges I faced were manifold: complex licensing processes, a labor law that hardly any employer in the country adhered to, the lack of basic IT infrastructure, a shortage of qualified personnel to hire and train, and, worst of all, another war.

I was trying to do something different, something no one had done in Eritrea: export locally developed software.

Blame it on age, inexperience, or pure immaturity, but nowhere did I mention "war economy" in my business plan.

To begin with, the scope of the project changed almost at once. The scope of our proposal was limited to the automation of the Commercial Bank of Eritrea. But, upon our arrival, we learned that the Department of Macro Policy, which was coordinating the national development initiatives in collaboration with the National Bank of Eritrea, decided to add the Commercial Bank of Eritrea to a larger initiative of developing an integrated banking system for all four banks in Eritrea: the

National Bank of Eritrea, the Commercial Bank, the Housing Bank, and the Development and Investment Bank. To that end, the Department of Macro Policy and the National Bank of Eritrea opened up the bidding process to now include other international firms.

Our team, newly operating in the country, tried to compensate for our lack of prior history of doing business with the government by offering to conduct a baseline study of the existing manual process at the Commercial Bank—pro bono. This study, which we undertook with full support of the general manager of the Commercial Bank of Eritrea, helped us in two ways: it allowed us to understand how the financial institutions in Eritrea operated, and it helped us prepare a tailor-made proposal that addressed the unique challenges Eritrean banks were facing. Considering we were there to train and to provide 24-7 live technical support to the banks, we hoped the Department of Macro Policy would meet us halfway and take a chance on us.

Unfortunately, that was not to be. The Department of Macro Policy and the Eritrean National Bank decided to go with KPMG, a US-based international consulting firm, as the firm had a proven track record in the financial industry as well as a name brand, while we did not. This created a serious obstacle to our moving forward. I had heard someone say, "If you want to understand a man, find out what his boss wants him to do." I was sure my financier and ardent supporter Mike Bloomberg had sponsored me so that I could help others to help themselves. Thus, I decided to look for other opportunities, this time concentrating more on high-end software application development training.

We submitted both technical and financial proposals to a few ministries, and the Ministry of Information invited us for a meeting. At the initial meeting, Zemihret Yohannes, the acting minister of information at the time, responded by stating that he liked and appreciated our technical proposal, and he thought the proposed fee was fair considering what the ministry would have to pay if they were to send a few individuals abroad to get similar training. But, he said, they just did not have the required funding and they might have to cancel the project.

Since the objective was to concentrate on knowledge transfer while looking for ways to generate revenue, we decided to take on the project at a nominal fee, less than 10 percent of the proposed cost.

Only three weeks after we started our training, the truce between Eritrea and Ethiopia came to an end. On May 12, 2000, the Ethiopian government reignited its offensive, declaring an all-out war across the more than a thousand kilometers of border between Eritrea and Ethiopia. Something that began as a border conflict turned into an invasion of a smaller nation. This was similar to Iraq's invasion of Kuwait, except in this case Eritreans were left on their own, back to a struggle for survival. No one from the international community sided with Eritrea. Ethiopia is such a valuable ally of the superpowers that "minor" blunders, such as invasion of an independent neighboring state, could easily be overlooked.

The international media's characterization of the conflict was that the Ethiopian government wanted only to regain a few border towns Eritrea had supposedly taken by force. Some even trivialized the conflict by describing it as "two bald men fighting for a comb."

On the ground, however, within a week the Ethiopian army was crawling over at least a third of Eritrea's land. The war was unfolding only sixty miles away from Asmara. The way they were handling the "border conflict" made it appear that the Ethiopians had changed their minds on accepting Eritrea's independence, which had been settled in 1993 through a UN-supervised referendum.

This was the environment in which we held our first training.

When the war reached its peak, Western countries decided to airlift their citizens out of Eritrea. The US Embassy made house calls to all US citizens and informed us that a plane had been chartered to take us to Germany. We were given instructions to come to the Intercontinental Hotel near the airport. I had already decided I would not leave Eritrea at that time. I did not believe that many Eritrean expatriates would leave, either.

I went to the Intercontinental Hotel to assess the situation. When I saw the people in the lobby of the five-star hotel, preparing to leave the country, my mind went off on a tangent. I compared the people in the lobby to the picture of young men and women I had seen running toward the trucks heading to the battle front that day. Some of those young men and women were my childhood friends, my schoolmates, and my relatives who just happened to be in the city on medical leave, family leave, or vacation leave, or were—in some cases—absent without leave. When the radio announced the resumption of war, however, they all rushed to the front line, like a colony of bees whose honeycomb had been attacked.

I compared the two pictures. The difference between the two groups seemed to me to be a matter of each person's self-valuation. I then asked myself two questions: "How much more is my life worth than the youngsters here?" and "What is my guarantee that I am going to live to see tomorrow?" The difference is a matter of mind-set. Which one takes the center stage? The *I* for self or the *we* for community?

I went back to my office, hoping that my presence might add some minuscule value to the morale and confidence of my compatriots.

A couple of days later, one of my old friends was passing through Asmara and called me at the office. When I picked up the phone, his first words were, "I'm so glad you didn't embarrass us." His unit was rushing toward the central front, and he had just stopped at a shop nearby to call and confirm that I had not fled the country. At that moment, I felt proud that I had not fled my birth country and left my compatriots at that crucial time in the nation's history. I don't think I would have been able to live with myself had I left.

At the time, Iyoba, my best friend from childhood, was moving from the Assab front to the central front. I remembered playing with him on the monkey bars before elementary school, but now he was a man going off to war.

This move was to stop the wave of the Ethiopian army trying to penetrate through the central front to reach Asmara. The border is a few miles away from the capital at those spots, and the Ethiopians got within sixty miles by focusing their attack through the center of the country, taking the shortest route from the border. From where we were, we could easily hear the sounds of heavy mortars and artilleries.

From the way the Ethiopian army was conducting the war, it had become clear that Ethiopia's true intent was to once again annex Eritrea, using the border war as a pretext.

As the former US Ambassador to Ethiopia David Shinn later reluctantly acknowledged:

> "I would point out one thing that was mentioned to me on several occasions on meetings that I had with Prime Minister Meles [Zenawi], which I always found fascinating, and I was never able to sort of get from him why he made those statements. But on several occasions during the conflict, the 1998–2000 conflict, he said, "Mr. Ambassador, one of these days we are going to be back together again," and I would try to press on that to find out, how is this going to happen? What's the plan here? He gave no time frame at all and he did not imply it would happen in his lifetime, but he made that statement on several occasions to me, and I found it intriguing but was never able to determine why he thought that was going to happen. But I am convinced he believed it very sincerely."[39]

Eritreans had repeatedly tried to convince the international community that Ethiopia's declaration of war against Eritrea had nothing to do with a border dispute. The border between Eritrea and Ethiopia is said to be one of the most well-defined borders on the continent of Africa—Menelik

---

39 Ethiopia–Eritrea relations conference, October 18, 2015, hosted by Ethiopia Vision and ESAT (Ethiopian Satellite TV).

of Ethiopia and the Italian colonizers of Eritrea had defined or delimited that border unambiguously through the treaties they signed in 1900, 1902, and 1908.

At any rate, using the border conflict as a pretext, on May 12, 2000, Ethiopia opened an all-out war on the nascent nation.

The Ethiopians started attacking through the central front, the shortest distance to Asmara. Within a few days, they were able to gain about twenty miles of land, though they suffered tens of thousands of casualties. This appeared to mirror the strategy Germany had used in World War I. Initially, tens of thousands of Ethiopian soldiers had been sent to the land mine–infested Eritrean defense lines. The booby traps were cleared only by each land mine killing one or more Ethiopian soldiers, most likely unfortunate souls who had been conscripted from among the poorest sections of Ethiopian society, in the southern region. According to accounts given by prisoners of war, there were units within the Ethiopian army whose sole task was to bury the "land mine deflectors," in order to preserve the morale of the remaining soldiers. Once the booby traps were cleared with the sacrifice of tens of thousands of lives, more soldiers were sent en masse to the Eritrean front line, turning the area into Africa's latest killing fields. The Eritrean army stationed in the central front fought till they started to run out of bullets and ammunition. Once they understood Ethiopia's military strategy—complete willingness to pay whatever human cost was necessary to capture the Eritrean capital city—Eritrea's military leadership decided on a strategic withdrawal.

As the Eritrean military units on the central front systematically withdrew, while slowing down the surge of the Ethiopian army during the weekend of May 20, my friend Iyoba's unit was coming up from the southern front to replace units that had been fighting for seven days without a break. Some divisions from the southern front came by cargo plane, while others drove for more than twenty hours to get to the front line.

Once Corps 491 arrived, an Ethiopian general named Samora Yonus is reported to have said in a radio communication to his commanders, "Forget it now; the mosquitoes of the Sahara have arrived." Members of Corps 491 earned that nickname because the unit had been stationed in the deserts of the southern front since the day the Ethiopian parliament declared war on Eritrea in 1998. The unit was by this time battle hardened.

Supported by long-range artillery and multiple rocket launchers, Corps 491 gave the Ethiopian army what a religious fanatic might call God's wrath—total annihilation. General Samora Yonus's prophetic declaration of defeat and despair came true. The Ethiopian army realized the capture of Asmara was not to be, and their leaders appeared to face the grim facts: there was no way for them to get to Asmara. The only thing left to gain would be more dead bodies, and they'd had more than enough of that. So they went to their second option: capture the Red Sea port of Assab, on the southern front. Convinced that a great number of the mosquitoes of the Sahara were now stranded in the central front, they convinced themselves they would have an easy ride to Assab.

The limited number of divisions of Corps 491 that remained fought vehemently to safeguard the port city while strategically withdrawing from their front line, about fifty miles from Assab. They continued fighting while waiting for the arrival of their comrades.

The Corps 491 divisions that had traveled hundreds of miles to the central front had to return to the south. Some squeezed into the limited number of cargo planes like broods of chickens, while others traveled atop armored personnel carriers and other ground transport.

By the time they got there, the units that remained had withdrawn to less than ten miles from the port city. But once all the units of Corps 491 and other units from central and western fronts arrived in Assab, the momentum of the war changed, and within twenty hours the Ethiopian army was pushed all the way back to the border, some fifty miles from the port of Assab. This front, too, was littered with dead bodies. What made this a worse spectacle compared to the central front was that the Assab front is an open desert, while the central front had mountains and trees that at least could conceal the scope of the massacre.

About a week later, the same old friend who called to check if I had left Eritrea called again. I asked him about Iyoba's whereabouts. He paused at first and then said, "He didn't make it."

Iyoba was martyred on May 23, 2000, at Adi-Begio.

I was not sure how to react to the news. I believed Iyoba knew that he was not going to make it back alive. The last time Iyoba and I had spoken was when he phoned me from the port of Assab. We'd talked for about an hour about the looming war. Ethiopia's preparation for an all-out war was an open secret; everyone knew they had been purchasing Sukhoi Su-27 fighter planes, super-maneuverable Russian-made twin-engine aircrafts. The Ethiopian military was arming itself to the teeth with heavy armaments purchased using aid funds. Western countries were providing financial assistance to Ethiopia for the eradication of the episodic droughts and famine that have wreaked havoc on that country. And yet the Ethiopian government was spending the funds on military armaments for the invasion of a neighboring country.

After hearing of Iyoba's martyrdom, I decided to visit Akberet Gebrehiwet, Iyoba's aunt on his mother's side, to inquire about the fate of his two brothers. After exchanging the customary greetings, I asked Akberet if there was any news of Robel or Demsas, Iyoba's brothers. Akberet told me that her sister Dehab had heard that Robel had been wounded and taken to the makeshift hospital in Filfil-Solomuna, in the northern part of the Red Sea region. Dehab had also informed Akberet that she was planning to go there if she found a way. I told Akberet I would try to go to Filfil-Solomuna and find out for sure if Robel was actually there, and promised I would let her know what I found out.

There was no word of Demsas's whereabouts. I later contacted some members of his unit, and the most reliable information I obtained was that Demsas had gone across the Ethiopian frontier with the military intelligence team and nothing had been heard of him since.

I now had to find a way to travel to the hospital in Filfil-Solomuna. It was time for me to search my virtual database for the names of those close to me. It did not take long before my virtual search result returned with Zemihret Yohannes, the acting minister of information and one of the people—along with his deputy, Azeb Tewolde, the director of the Research and Documentation Center—to whom I turned for advice, guidance, and moral support when needed.

Zemihret Yohannes helped me get a permit that would allow me to travel to the Northern Red Sea administrative zone. After getting the permit, I started contemplating the next challenge: How would I get to Filfil-Solomuna? I had no idea. Then I thought of people who might possibly know the area. I was fairly certain my cousin Asmerom Mengisteab would know the place. I found Asmerom in his office at the Department of Environment under the Ministry of Land, Water, and Environment and asked him if he knew how to get to the hospital at Filfil-Solomuna. He said he had been there once and that the place could be reached through one of two ways. Well, my next question for Asmerom was could he go with me the next day. Without any hesitation, my cousin said yes, and he asked me the reason that was so urgent that it had to be done the next day. I briefly told him the story of Robel. Asmerom said we would need a four-wheel drive or similar heavy-duty vehicle. I left his office saying that I would see him the next day at nine a.m. in his office.

I asked my uncle Zemuy Habte to let me borrow his four-wheel-drive Opel. My uncle told me to pick up the car the next day at eight a.m. at a coffee shop in downtown Asmara.

I went to see Biniam Tesfagabir Hizbay, Iyoba's first cousin. I found Biniam in his house and told him the fate of his cousins. I also told Biniam that I was planning to go to Filfil-Solomuna the next day with my cousin Asmerom. Biniam said he would be happy to go with us and asked me to pick him up the next morning.

Until this day, all I knew about Filfil-Solomuna or the Northern Red Sea was the area's historical significance. The Northern Red Sea was the base of the Eritrean People's Liberation Front in the 1970s. To me, the place might as well be in Sahel, the northernmost part of Eritrea.

I picked up Asmerom and Biniam early in the morning. We drove to one of the bakeries in downtown Asmara and purchased loaves of bread and bottles of water for our trip. Based on Asmerom's guidance, we started heading toward the northern part of the city, passing Cicero soccer stadium. We stopped at the city limit, entering Adi-Abeyto, to ask for directions. I put my head out of the window and asked a young man who was standing next to a bus stop sign, "Hi. Can you tell me how we can get to Filfil-Solomuna?"

The guy looked around, perhaps wondering if I was crazy. He then stared back at me and said no while shaking his head.

Asmerom then leaned forward and said, "What about Bahri?"[40]

"Uh. Why didn't you say so, then. Go straight and make a right turn when you get to Serejaqa. That road will take you to the Northern Red Sea." This was great information—it gave us a reference of a town that we could ask people about on our way.

With the innocence of an urban upbringing and with a great deal of concern about getting lost, we decided to stop and

40 The locals use the term *Bahri* (sea) to refer to the Northern Red Sea regional administration.

ask for directions once we reached the next town, Embaderho. We hadn't driven far from Asmara, but we thought we would do better asking than getting lost in unfamiliar places.

At Embaderho, we found a guy in military clothing standing in front of a shop and asked him for directions. This time I made sure I used the right term, Bahri. The guy told us to make a right turn immediately after we passed a small river surrounded by a bunch of trees.

After driving for about twenty minutes more, we got concerned and decided to stop and ask an older man standing on the other side of the road waiting for the bus heading to Asmara. He told us we had passed the road and pointed his fingers down the hill we'd just come through and told us we needed to turn left. There was no road we could see. After getting more clarification, we could see some unpaved dirt road that we thought was used by the residents of the nearby villages. Apparently, that was our road.

Not long after we left the main road, we found a part of the road completely covered with rocks and sharp stones. I kept switching between first and second gear. We finally got onto a dirt road passing through the farmlands of Afdeyu, Kwandoba, Deqseb, Guritat, and other villages in the Karneshim subzone.

After driving through the plains of Karneshim, we were welcomed by the amazing site of coffee and fruit plantations at Sabur and the serene beauty of the Northern Red Sea. The thousand-year-old forest was breathtaking. We looked as far as our eyes could allow, but all we could see were hills and rings of mountains completely covered by forest. Most of the plantation was on our right side, while both sides of the road down the hill were covered with giant trees. The branches of some of the trees spanned multiple turns of the road.

The beauty of the Northern Red Sea's scenery took me back to the Loch Raven Reservoir in Baltimore, one of my favorite places during my college years. In addition to visiting the Inner Harbor, driving through the hills of Loch Raven Drive, walking across the bridges, and trekking through the various trails of Loch Raven Reservoir was one of my favorite pastimes in Baltimore. The waters in Baltimore were beautiful, but they were nothing compared to the breathtaking beauty of the Northern Red Sea, which could easily take anyone to nirvana.

On a normal trip to the area, we would have a lot of things to talk about. My childhood friend Biniam and I had a lot to catch up on since our time together in school. But not at that moment.

Asmerom was my cousin from Adi-Hayo. Asmerom and I could have talked about family matters. We could also have talked about the historical significance of the place. The lush forest of the Northern Red Sea protected and sheltered the Eritrean freedom fighters. We could have asked the forest to tell us the secrets of the fallen heroes it had kept for many years. I was certain the forest had an amazing story to tell. The forest needed the heroes of the Eritrean freedom fight for its survival, and the heroes needed the forest for theirs. Each played its role so well that they both survived. The relationship between a host and parasite, where each is one and the same, would make a great story for many books.

But at that moment, we all were silent. Fear of the unknown had taken full control of the three of us. What was the fate of Robel? Was his injury life threatening? Would he make it? Could we make it in time to see him alive? Would we even make it there safely? Too many questions for any of us to answer. The best option was to remain silent. I at least had the luxury of focusing on driving with caution so that we didn't roll down the mountain, where our bones would break into pieces too small for anyone to recognize.

Not long after we passed Sabur and started descending, reality hit us hard when I heard an odd cranking noise. My blood pressure went up—I thought the car was broken. I panicked and stopped the car. I turned off the ignition and the three of us got out. I was prepared for anything. Knowing very little about cars, it would not have surprised me if the engine had shut off because of the ups and downs of the rough terrain. Luckily, Asmerom saw that the front passenger-side tire was flat. That was a huge relief.

While we were changing the tire, a middle-aged man in military attire and carrying an AK-47 on his shoulder came down the hill and toward us. After we exchanged the usual warm greetings, he asked us why we were there. From his tone, it was clear to us that there hadn't been that many civilians traveling through that part of the country. The rough terrain we were driving on was also another testimonial for how little the road had been used in the past. We handed him our permit and told him we were heading toward the makeshift hospital in Filfil-Solomuna. After reading the letter, he told us to be very careful of the forking service roads on our way. He told us to avoid the road going to Fishey Mirara and to bear right at every fork we encountered. He also told us to look for tents and military camps on our side once we got down the hill, which he estimated might take us a couple of hours.

After driving with a great deal of concern and anxiety about encountering more flat tires or other damage to the vehicle, and at the same time enjoying the mesmerizing scenery and the natural beauty of Northern Red Sea, we passed Filfil and arrived in Solomuna around five in the afternoon. We turned right once we saw the military camps at Solomuna and parked our car in front of a three-room building that appeared to be the headquarters of the camp.

We walked into the building and asked the officer sitting behind the desk for assistance. We exchanged warm greetings, and I said meekly, "I was told my brother Robel was transferred here for medical treatment. I was wondering if you could help us find him."

"Can I see your ID, please?" the officer responded.

I handed him my Eritrean national ID. He scanned the ID and said, "Your name says Dawit Gebremichael Habte, and you claimed Robel Tsehaye Hizbay was your brother. It is not adding up. Why did you say Robel is your brother?" I could see in the officer's face that he was getting irate. He started flipping my ID back and forth.

I guessed it was time to start telling him the whole story. "Listen, we might not have the same mother or father, but Robel is my brother. Robel is my best friend's older brother. Iyoba, his younger brother, did not make it. He was martyred in Adi-Begio. We have not heard of Demsas, Robel's older brother, for the past three weeks. The only information we have is that Demsas and his intelligence unit have gone behind enemy lines at the Assab front and, so far, nothing has been heard of them. Their father passed away when they were kids, and their mother lives in Saudi Arabia. Now, why don't you tell me which one of them is not my brother?" I pointed to Biniam, who was standing on my left side. "This guy is their cousin. His name is Biniam Tesfagabir Hizbay."

The officer glanced at Biniam and flipped my ID and said, "Am I reading this right? Do you live in the US? You actually came all the way here from the US?"

"That is right," I said.

He gave me back my ID card and gave a note to one of his colleagues to announce Robel's name on the microphone tied to a pole standing in the middle of the camp. He also asked his colleague to get us tea.

Seconds later, we heard a loud voice asking Robel Tsehaye Hizbay to come to the headquarters immediately. The announcement was repeated every other minute, and finally a young man with wounded leg limped into the room and said, "Who is looking for Robel? Robel was transferred to Ala earlier today."

"Are you sure we are talking about the same Robel? We were told he was here," I said.

"I don't know. I only know of Robel wedi-Keren. We were in the same unit, division thirty-two."

"Yup, that is him," I confirmed. "You guys were stationed by the Zalambessa front."

Robel was widely known by his nickname, wedi-Keren— the son of Keren—which he acquired because he lived with his maternal grandmother in the town of Keren for most of his life.

Robel's comrade confirmed that we were talking about the same man. He told us Robel had been treated for a wound on his shoulder and transferred to Ala for follow-up and to get released to his unit. He assured us Robel was well and we might even see him soon, considering the doctors in Ala would likely send him home for rest and recovery.

It was nearing nightfall, and we needed to leave before it became too dark. We thanked our hosts and asked them for the best way to get back to Asmara. They told us we should be able to get back on the paved road connecting Asmara and the port city of Massawa. For our safety, the officer organized a unit of about twenty personnel to drive with us till we got to a paved road. They all jumped onto an armored truck. The truck started leaving the camp with some of the soldiers sitting in the cab with the driver and the rest in the back, next to the armor that was ready to be used at any minute. We followed them till we reached a place called Metkel-Abiet, where we made a right turn on the asphalt road heading toward Gahtielay. We waved our farewells to each other and the truck made a U-turn.

It had already gotten too dark for us to drive more than seventy kilometers on the mountainous and snakelike road leading to Asmara. Instead, we decided to spend the night in Massawa and get back home the next day.

We left Massawa early in the morning and we arrived in Asmara around nine a.m. I dropped Asmerom at his office and Biniam at his house and drove to Akberet Gebrehiwet's house to tell her the good news. Akberet was elated to hear of Robel's well-being.

As Robel later told me, he was hit by an explosive shell fired by the Ethiopian army on May 21, 2000. The larger part of the shell hit my cousin Michael Haile from Adi-Hayo. What was news to me was that Robel and Michael were actually close friends. According to Robel, in one of their conversations Michael mentioned that he hailed from Adi-Hayo. Robel asked Michael if he knew my parents. Considering the size of Adi-Hayo and the unity of the village, Michael told him we knew each other and we were in fact cousins. Unfortunately, thanks to this bloody war, I never had a chance to talk to my friend and my cousin together while they were both alive. I had to hear from my friend that the largest part of the exploding Ethiopian shell hit my cousin, who died on the spot, and the remaining part hit my friend, who was able to reach hospital for treatment, gaining an extension on his lease to live on this earth.

Two weeks later, Demsas sent a message from Assab informing his aunt Akberet that he was well. As the norm of military life dictated, Demsas just said he was not able to communicate to his aunt because he was on an assignment that had lasted longer than he'd anticipated.

When one examined the trajectory of this senseless war, it was easy to identify significant differences between the Ethiopian and Eritrean armed forces. The Ethiopian army was filled with soldiers who mainly came from the disadvantaged sections of the Ethiopian society—the Oromo group, to be specific. The elite Ethiopians occupied the leadership and political offices and led the war effort from a safe distance. The Eritrean fighters, on the other hand, were either former freedom fighters or national service conscripts, who at times were from the same families. For Eritreans, the war touched each and every household. Some affluent families lost three or four children. More than fifteen of my friends, classmates, and other children I grew up with paid the ultimate price to defend Eritrea.

Our grandfathers' and our fathers' generations sacrificed their entire lives for the independence of the nation, and my generation preserved it.

According to the scriptures, when Goliath arrived to the battleground, "He had a bronze helmet on his head and wore a coat of scale armor of bronze weighing five thousand shekels; on his legs he wore bronze greaves, and a bronze javelin was slung on his back. His spear shaft was like a weaver's rod, and its iron point weighed six hundred shekels."[41] David, on the other hand, went to the battlefield with five smooth stones he picked from the stream in the pouch of his shepherd's bag and his sling in his hand. David did not run into Goliath like a boxer would jump into the MMA cage or a professional wrestler would into the wrestling ring. Instead, David defeated Goliath by slinging his stone and striking the giant on the forehead.

Eritreans defeated one of Africa's largest and most heavily equipped armies for a second time by strategically withdrawing and attacking at the place and time of their choosing. Once the Ethiopian political leadership accepted the futility of their latest round of military adventurism and realized that they could not reverse Eritrea's independence by force, they were forced to sign the Agreement on Cessation of Hostilities on June 18, 2000. The Agreement on Cessation of Hostilities

41 1 Samuel 17:5-7, New International Version.

became the basis for the Algiers Agreement, the peace agreement Eritrea and Ethiopia signed on December 12, 2000, agreeing to take their case to the Permanent Court of Arbitration. The Algiers Agreement established the Eritrea–Ethiopia Boundary Commission (EEBC), a neutral commission mandated "to delimit and demarcate the colonial treaty border based on pertinent colonial treaties (1900, 1902, and 1908) and applicable international law." The "final and binding" agreement was witnessed and guaranteed by Secretary General Kofi Annan representing the United Nations, Secretary of State Madeleine Albright representing the United States, Secretary-General Salim Ahmed Salim representing the OAU (the predecessor of the African Union), Senator Renato Serri representing the European Union, President Abdelaziz Bouteflika of the Democratic Republic of Algeria, and President Olusegun Obasanjo of Nigeria.[42]

The border commission rendered its decision on April 13, 2002. Initially, both countries accepted the decision. But on September 19, 2003, Ethiopia informed the Security Council that it had rejected the commission's decision because the commission had awarded the town of Badme, the flashpoint of the conflict, to Eritrea.[43]

42 Agreement Between the Government of the Federal Democratic Republic of Ethiopia and the Government of Eritrea, December 12, 2000.

43 Ethiopia's letter to the Security Council can be found at http://www.ethiomedia.com/press/meles_un_letter_091903.html. The letter dated October 7, 2003, from the president of the Eritrea–Ethiopia Boundary Commission to the secretary-general responding to Ethiopia's letter, can be found at http://dehai.org/demarcation-watch/articles/EEBC-Oct-7-2003-letter.pdf.

The US and other international negotiators failed to push for an equitable solution. Craig Calhoun, the former director of the London School of Economics and Political Science, accurately summarized the US government and the international community's handling of the conflict between Eritrea and Ethiopia: "US diplomatic interventions were largely incompetent and counterproductive, led by an inexperienced political appointee instead of an experienced diplomat. International mediators have failed largely because they have called for a return to the status quo ante bellum defined in Ethiopia's favor as that which existed on May 5, rather than taking into account the colonial boundary that the Eritreans believe should define the border."[44]

To make matters worse, instead of enforcing the Permanent Court of Arbitration's ruling, in flagrant violation of international norms and principles, inquisitors at the US Department of State African desk wanted to appease Ethiopia by reversing the "final and binding" 2002 Eritrea–Ethiopia Boundary Commission decision.

In his memoir *Surrender Is Not an Option*, former US Ambassador to the UN John Bolton states, "For reasons I never understood, however, Frazer reversed course, and asked in early February [2006] to reopen the 2002 EEBC decision, which she had concluded was wrong, and award a major piece of disputed territory to Ethiopia. I was at a loss how to explain that to the Security Council, so I didn't..."[45] Jendayi Frazer

44 Calhoun, Craig, "Ethiopia's Ethnic Cleansing," *Dissent*, Winter 1999, p. 47-50.

45 Bolton, John, *Surrender Is Not an Option: Defending America at the United Nations,* New York: Simon & Schuster, 2007, p. 347-8.

was the US assistant secretary of state for African Affairs under George W. Bush's administration.[46]

The border demarcation that was supposed to be completed six months after the boundary commission rendered its decision on April 13, 2002, had been postponed indefinitely. At the time of this writing, the border between Eritrea and Ethiopia has yet to be physically demarcated.

As long as the border remains undemarcated, tension between both countries will remain, and unless steps are taken to solve it, war may follow. The last thing the region needs is another war. The Algiers Peace Agreement was guaranteed by the UN, the US, the EU, and the African Union. The guarantors have a responsibility at least to the people of the region to ensure that the border is demarcated.

President John F. Kennedy once said, "If there is any current trend toward meeting present problems with old clichés, this is the moment to stop it—before it lands us all in a bog of sterile acrimony." Consistently, the centuries-old US and European foreign policies based on protecting the fictitious "Christian island surrounded by a sea of Islam" help neither the Ethiopians nor the other people of the region. Staying the course of repeating historical follies is not going to help or advance any country's national interest. It definitely does not and will not help the people of the region.

Ethiopians, for their part, need to fully understand that the Eritrea that was illegally and forcefully annexed to

---

46 Incidentally, Ethiopia received 100 percent relief on all debt incurred by the country prior to January 1, 2005. Merely five years after invading its neighbor and flagrantly defying international laws and norms, suddenly Ethiopia became a "low risk of external debt distress," according to the IMF, the World Bank, and the rest of the international organizations.

Ethiopia in 1962 is no more. At the same time, irrespective of their historical misgivings and the repeated miscarriages of justice rendered upon them by the international community, Eritreans need to look forward to their peaceful coexistence with Ethiopians, their neighbors to the south. Both Eritreans and Ethiopians need to look forward to realizing the intrinsic and instrumental values of the peace dividend.

With regard to NATNA Business Solutions, during the years I stayed in Eritrea, from August 1999 through December 2003, we made substantial progress in terms of infrastructure and human resources development.

We developed and integrated enterprise resource planning software and provided training for the Ministry of Finance. We designed, developed, and implemented software for the National Commission for the Demobilization and Reintegration Program to ensure that hundreds of thousands of former combatants were successfully integrated into civilian life. We also assumed the responsibility of full IT training at user and professional support levels for staff members, ensuring readily available and sustainable technical support for two years.

We provided the Department of Environment of the Ministry of Land, Water, and Environment with full networking deployment and trained the supporting staff on networking setup and configuration. We also provided training on environmental information management including data collection, storage, and management, using the internet to gather information related to environmental biodiversity, climate change, and accessing environmental Listservs and discussion groups. But the real legacy of NATNA exists in those that we introduced to technology solutions.

I met one of our first trainees in Asmara a year or so before I left Eritrea and came back to the US. We exchanged the customary greetings, and he insisted on buying me coffee. I accepted his invitation and we sat outside a local place called American Bar. The man then started to thank me, saying, "Thanks to the training now all I have to do is click on the formulas and equations I have written in Excel and I get the monthly, quarterly, and annual financial statements in seconds. Before, I used to prepare the financial statements manually using a calculator. I used Excel for storage only. A few months ago, the ministry gave me three members of the National Service, and I'm now showing them how to prepare the financial statements so I can concentrate on other things."

I was surprised. I remembered letting him go from the training, after he attended for merely four weeks, because he did not do well on his last exam. I now realized that he was actually implementing what he had learned at a faster rate than some of the students who had taken the full six-month course. I reflected on my own junior hire training at Bloomberg and on the fact that I had failed the final finance exam the first time I took it, passing it only on the second try. I knew that did not make me any less of a qualified financial software developer.

On that day, I saw a new dilemma for our project. Whom should we invest in most: the dedicated and hardworking students who lacked the academic background in the subject matter—but had spent their precious youth in the trenches fighting for the freedom that the hotshot students were then able to enjoy—or the ones with solid academic backgrounds who need to be the change agents in the country?

It was time to reassess our approach and try to make our training programs as inclusive as possible. From then on I decided to let each group of students stay together till the end of the training period, irrespective of their grades, realizing that even the ones with lower grades would be able to pick up at least one or two concepts from each lecture or lab.

Another one of my trainees is worth mentioning here. He was from a town called Mendefera. The young man in his late twenties had been referred to our training program a couple of years previously by one of the first programmers we trained and hired. When our programmer introduced me to the young man, she told me he had been teaching elementary school before entering the National Service. As the border conflict with Ethiopia had started during the young man's tour of duty with the National Service, he was sent to the southern front to join the regular army. At the end of the war, the young man was relieved from military duty because he was the only child to his father and mother. I told him to register and start training with the next batch, and that he did not have to worry about the fee as long as he had a place to stay in the city.

He finished his six-month training and told me he planned to convert his father's minishop to a computer training center. He asked if I could help him. I allowed him to borrow or make copies of the books and training materials we had and told him to let me know if there was anything else I could do to help. As a demonstration of his dedication, in a few months the young man came to the office with some documents and a draft of a loan application. I gave him my suggestions, and he submitted his proposal and application to the Development and Investment Bank. The bank accepted the application for the purchase of twelve computers, using the hardware as collateral. He also obtained his license with our recommendation of his technical capabilities, and he had soon converted his father's shop into an IT training center. I wondered at the time what his father—who was risking the only means of income for his family—thought of the big gamble his son was undertaking.

A couple of years later, the young man came to Asmara with his father and mother and invited me to have lunch with them at a local restaurant. I accepted their invitation with the apology that I should have been the one to come to Mendefera. I told the father that my admiration and respect for his son was beyond limit. I also told him I never heard of a father who would risk his family's only source of income so that his son could experiment with a technology the father did not understand. During the meal the young man's father told me what he was thinking on this subject—and his explanation increased even more my respect for him.

He said, "You see, I have no idea of technology or anything of that sort. I can barely read or write. All I know is how to get some coffee, sugar, bread, and soft drinks from the wholesalers and sell them to my neighbors. My only son came and told me he wanted to convert my shop into a training center. He tried to explain to me about the training he took. Even though I may not know about technology and the other stuff, I know for sure the world is for the future generation, not for us, the older ones. As such, I decided to take a chance on my son."

In the journey we call life, I cannot claim to have taken the road less traveled, like the traveler in Robert Frost's poem. Frost's "The Road Not Taken" was one of my favorite poems in college. The poem goes as follows:

> *Two roads diverged in a yellow wood,*
> *And sorry I could not travel both*
> *And be one traveler, long I stood*
> *And looked down one as far as I could*
> *To where it bent in the undergrowth;*
> *Then took the other, as just as fair,*
> *And having perhaps the better claim,*
> *Because it was grassy and wanted wear;*
> *Though as for that the passing there*
> *Had worn them really about the same,*
> *And both that morning equally lay*
> *In leaves no step had trodden black.*
> *Oh, I kept the first for another day!*
> *Yet knowing how way leads on to way,*
> *I doubted if I should ever come back.*
> *I shall be telling this with a sigh*
> *Somewhere ages and ages hence:*
> *Two roads diverged in a wood, and I—*
> *I took the one less traveled by,*
> *And that has made all the difference.*

When Frost's traveler reached the two divergent roads, the traveler appears to have made a conscious decision to take the road less traveled by. This deliberate choice would seem to have paid off, considering it "made all the difference." In my case, meeting the individuals who crossed my path was purely coincidental and happened through sheer luck. I did not make any conscious choice; I merely encountered them along the way. I stumbled from one Good Samaritan to another; each became a rung on the ladder of my youth. I did, however, make a conscious effort to hold on to whatever help each Good Samaritan offered, and that truly seems to have made all the difference.

Consistent to the old time-tested Eritrean adage "To those who have done you favors, either return the favor or tell others about their good deeds," I hope I have conveyed the essence of the deeds of each Good Samaritan.

The love and support we received from Aya Ande Chirum and the residents of Adi-Hayo, my ancestral village, is a confirmation of the popular saying "It takes a village to raise a child."

Aboy Mebrahtu Negusse, Alembrhan and Dilinay Berhe, Mizan Ogbatzion, Asmerom Brhane, Samuel Tedros Gebru, and the rest of our neighbors in Gejeret gave us the foundations we needed at a very young and impressionable age. The city of Asmara in general and my birth place Gejeret in particular was the nirvana of our childhood.

Aya Mohammed Kelifa, Aboy Araya Weldehiwet, and Adey Leterbrhan Fsehaye's tender love and support is a testament to the true meaning of friendship. As Muhammad Ali, a.k.a. the Greatest, once said, "If you haven't learned the meaning of friendship, you really haven't learned anything."

Dr. Jack Dalton, Dave Rysak, Biff LeVee, Alan Zins, and the congregation of Ambassadors of Fourth Presbyterian Church did not only sponsor us to resettle in the United States but provided us the support and guidance we needed during our arrival and beyond. Their friendship throughout our life in the United States is a testament to the decency and good-heartedness of Americans as a society.

Professor Tekie Fessehatzion, Professor Ghideon Abay Asmerom, Professor Berhe Habte-Giorgis, Beatrice Newel, Carolyn Finegar, Cyrus Ishikawa, Rose Varner-Gaskins, and the rest of the educators became my guiding lights, my north stars, during my teenage and adult years.

Mike Bloomberg, one of the most influential entrepreneurs of the second half of the century, a philanthropist and public servant, crossed paths with a young African. Mike and I have nothing in common, and he had no reason to give me, a junior programmer, even a minute of his time. In fact, when our paths crossed, Mike, as the CEO and founder of the media giant Bloomberg LP, could have easily let himself pass with a polite smile and we both would have forgotten about each other. It would have been another episode of Mark Twain's *The Prince and the Pauper*, except, this time, the two strangers would pass each other without leaving any trace of the encounter. No memory of the path or the people. Nevertheless, Mike's character and his principle in investing in human beings, the belief he successfully instilled in me, brought us together.

Just like my parents during their prayers, I can only give gratitude in a low voice to the angels without wings, for a moment of silence is reserved for those selfless, faceless, and nameless heroes who sacrifice their precious lives for the survival and continuity of their respective societies.

ACKNOWLEDGMENTS

"Shallow men believe in luck. Strong men believe in cause and effect." —Ralph Waldo Emerson

Unlike Emerson, I believe that luck, especially good luck, has run all through the life of this shallow man. I would like to thank God for my luck and for affording me the opportunity to tell of the voyage of a life I could not have dreamed of.

I would also like to thank the following army of mortals for their continuous encouragement and unparalleled support in getting this book published:

My wife, Monaliza Zerabruck Tewelde, without whom it would not have been possible to write and publish a book while raising four free-spirited boys and an equally energetic daughter. For many years, a great portion of the family responsibility has been outsourced to Mom. Thank you.

My children, Mieron, Haben, Mathew Iyob, Jacob, and Laila Ruth, for the joy you bring to my life.

Dr. Ghideon Abay Asmerom, for standing beside me throughout the ten years it took to write this book. Dr. Ghideon reviewed and edited starting with the first fifty pages

I drafted in November 2005. He provided me with the guidance and support I dearly needed in getting this book to reach its readers.

The late Professor Tekie Fessehatzion, for his guidance in life and after life. Professor Tekie once told me that I had an "inspiring story in the making," but I had to work hard on the delivery. I wish he had lived to see the publication of this book.

Dr. Berhe Habte-Giorgis, for his continuous encouragement and support and for providing a wealth of information on Eritrean and Ethiopian history.

My high school counselor Beatrice Newel and my high school college and career adviser Carolyn Finegar, for their continuous support and encouragement throughout the making of this book.

Mary Lou, for the time she spent reviewing my original manuscript in its entirety and for her honest feedback. I would also like to acknowledge and thank Mary Lou for her utmost patience with my kids and their cousins Abraham, Delina, Noel, and Nathan. Over the years, Mary Lou has been giving lessons in writing and preparation for the SAT to my kids and their cousins.

Karen James Cody, for reviewing my draft manuscript and her unreserved and honest editorial feedback and support.

Theodor Boyd and Erigbe Andemeskel for taking the time to review the initial draft and for providing me with constructive feedback.

Daniel Abraha Tesfay for keeping me honest with some events in recent Eritrean history and some of the childhood memories. Daniel has a photographic memory. He can easily give someone a detailed description of each house and the people who live in Gejeret, the neighborhood where we grew up, with such accuracy it makes you wonder whether he has actually lived in rotation with the various families.

Benyam Solomon, for reviewing the final manuscript and providing me with very constructive yet reluctant feedback. Benyam is such a great friend that he will always give you at least two options by saying, "You can also leave it the way it is."

Stephen Isaacs of Bloomberg LP, for his unparalleled support in guiding me through the maze of the book publishing world. When I initially wrote Stephen an email asking for his availability to talk over the phone, his reply was, "Please call whenever is convenient for you." As a representative of Bloomberg Press, Stephen is probably one of the busiest editors in the industry. But he took a keen interest in my manuscript and accommodated my needs on my own terms. Thank you.

Dr. Ronald Goldfarb of Goldfarb & Associates, my lawyer, for his extraordinary negotiating skills. I simply found Ron to be a gem in his profession.

Arthur Klebanoff, Michelle Weyenberg, Hannah Bennett, Alexia Garaventa, Brian Skulnik, Corina Lupp, Peter Clark, and the rest of the RosettaBooks staff for providing a pro-author alternative option to the traditional publishing houses. Special thanks to Peter Clark, my editor, for his genuine interest in my story and for asking the many hard and toilsome editorial questions I never asked of myself over the years. In making *Gratitude in Low Voices*, Peter has truly created the proverbial lemonade out of lemons. Thank you for the continuous encouragement and support throughout the editorial process.

Gregory McCaffery, the CEO and president of Bloomberg BNA. I can imagine the scarcity and value of his time. Yet he has gone out of his way to check on the status of my book every time we run into each other in the pantry, hallways, and elevators. Thanks for caring. It meant a lot to me knowing you had my back.

Joe Breda, executive vice president for product and research and development, and David Greer, tech director for product access and e-commerce, my two managers, for their unwavering friendship and for providing me with the time and space I needed during the book acquisition and editorial process. Legend has it that on Wednesday, October 22, 2014, Mike Bloomberg was meeting with his direct reports and Bloomberg BNA senior management in New York City. During one of the breakout sessions, Mike wanted to challenge his memory and told his audience, "There was this guy from Eritrea we supported to go back to help his birth country. I don't know what happened to him or where he is. I don't remember his name." Joe Breda instinctively responded by saying, "I know who you're talking about it. His name is Dawit Habte and he still works for you. I will send you his name when I get back to the office." Joe emailed me from his phone that afternoon, saying, "I have a funny story involving you and Mike Bloomberg. I'm on a flight back to Arlington. I'll try to find you when I get there." I sent Mike a thank-you note after hearing what Joe had to say, and our reunion made possible the realization of this book.

Mike Bloomberg, I am humbled and grateful to have worked for you, to have met you and to have known you as a person. You have never failed to amaze me as a person and as a leader. Of all the people you meet daily, globally, you remembered this obscure programmer who at one point in your life crossed your path. Thank you for remembering me after many years and for being part of my life. Thank you for everything. You are my hero.